POEMS TO ENJOY

LITERARY HERITAGE

LITERATURE TO
ENJOY
STORIES TO ENJOY
POEMS TO ENJOY
PLAYS TO ENJOY
READINGS TO ENJOY

LITERATURE TO
REMEMBER
STORIES TO REMEMBER
POEMS TO REMEMBER
PLAYS TO REMEMBER
READINGS TO REMEMBER

POEMS
TO
ENJOY

DOROTHY PETITT

Professor of English
San Francisco State College
San Francisco, California

THE MACMILLAN COMPANY New York
COLLIER-MACMILLAN LIMITED London

ACKNOWLEDGMENTS

For permission to reprint copyright material in this volume, grateful acknowledgment is made to the following:

George Allen & Unwin, Ltd.: For "The Child in School" from *Flower Shadows* by Alan S. Lee. For "It is a pleasure" by Tachibana Akemi from *Anthology of Japanese Literature,* edited by Donald Keene.

Miss Louise Andrews: For "I Wish That My Room Had a Floor" by Gelett Burgess, from *A Century of Humorous Verse.*

Mrs. Rowena Bennett: For "The Witch of Willowby Wood" by Rowena Bennett.

Mr. Arna Bontemps: For "Dark Girl" from *Golden Slippers* by Arna Bontemps.

Brandt & Brandt: For "Abraham Lincoln" from *A Book of Americans* by Rosemary and Stephen Vincent Benét, Holt, Rinehart and Winston, Inc. Copyright 1933, by Rosemary and Stephen Vincent Benét. Reprinted by permission of Brandt & Brandt.

University of California Press: For "Minnows are helpless" by Lord Toshiyori and "A world of dew" by Issa, from *The Year of My Life, A Translation of Issa's Oraga Haru* by Nobuyuki Yuasa.

Colum, Padraic: For "An Old Woman of the Roads."

Corinth Books, Inc.: For "Brian O Linn" and "Mrs. McGrath" from *Irish Street Ballads* by Colm O Lochlainn © 1960, Corinth Books, Inc.

Curtis Brown, Ltd.: For "An old silent pond" by Basho, "How cool cut hay smells" by Boncho, "One man and one fly" and "If things were better" by Issa, "Frog-school competing" by Shiki, "O moon, why must you" by Koyo from *Cricket Songs.* Reprinted by permission of the Author, copyright © 1964 by Harry Behn. "Little Elegy" from *Nude Descending a Staircase* by X. J. Kennedy. Reprinted by permission of the Author, copyright © 1960 by X. J. Kennedy.

J. M. Dent & Sons, Ltd.: For "Ask Daddy, He Won't Know," "The Eel," "The Duck," "The Hippopotamus," "The Octopus," "The Pig," "The Sniffle," from *Family Reunion* by Ogden Nash.

(Acknowledgments continued on page 188)

For assistance in the preparation of this manuscript, the editor wishes to thank Miss Barbara Harr.

Illustrated by William Hofmann.

The Macmillan Company, New York
Collier-Macmillan Canada, Ltd., Toronto, Ontario
Printed in the United States of America

7H

CONTENTS

1 SOUNDS SHAPE POEMS 2

2 POEMS TELL STORIES 36

3 POEMS DESCRIBE 58

Animals 60

vi

People

Scenes

Haiku

4 POEMS EXPRESS FEELINGS 100

Bright and Dark Moods 102

viii

5 POEMS MAKE FUN

6   POEMS EXPRESS IDEAS   142

7 POEMS MEAN THEMSELVES AND SOMETHING MORE 158

To the Reader

These new and old poems are for you to enjoy. When you have read all of them, you may enjoy choosing which ones you like best.

Sometimes people like poems just for their sounds, without paying much attention to what the poems say. Most readers, though, enjoy poems both for their special sounds *and* for their meaning. Some poems tell stories about heroes or about ordinary people. Others describe animals, people, or scenes. Some poems tell how someone feels about something; others make fun or express interesting ideas. Often a poem says several things at once.

You and your classmates should be able to agree on the basic meaning of a poem. Yet some of you may have different, but equally true, ideas about additional meanings in the poem. Discussing these ideas is one more way to enjoy a poem.

May you enjoy the poems in this book
> Because they are new,
> Because they are old,
> Because the sounds please you,
> Because the subjects interest you.

Above all, may you enjoy the poems in this book because they help you discover what you feel and what you think
> About them,
> About the world,
> About yourself.

1

SOUNDS
SHAPE
POEMS

The world is full of sound. Rain hits a window pane; a pile driver rises and falls; waves come ashore. The most familiar sound of all is a human voice speaking.

Have you ever recognized someone's voice, even though you couldn't hear his words distinctly? What identified his voice for you? Since each voice has a characteristic individual sound pattern, perhaps you recognized the pattern of his voice.

The voice of each poem, too, has an individual sound pattern. The words of the complete poem rise and fall in some kind of rhythm. The poet chooses a rhythm to fit the subject of his poem. A poem about a galloping horse, for instance, should probably have a different rhythm from a poem about a prowling cat. What kind of rhythm would you suggest for either subject?

Other sound patterns besides rhythm may help to shape a poem. Sometimes the poet repeats the same words exactly. The repetition emphasizes what he is saying. Sometimes he repeats the same sounds. He may repeat rhyming sounds, or he may repeat letter sounds at the beginning of words or inside words. Repetition of words and of sounds helps to connect the words of a poem to each other.

Because the words in a poem are closely connected in some kind of pattern, you are likely to pay close attention to their meaning. The poet has chosen his words carefully to focus his thought and feeling. He has paid attention both to what words mean and to how they sound together.

The first time you read a poem is like meeting a new friend. You just begin to get acquainted. But then, if you notice how sounds shape the poem, you may discover meanings you missed in the first reading. You may also find that you remember many of the word combinations. Sometimes readers memorize a complete poem without even trying.

Why might you want to remember the exact words someone says to you? Why might you want to remember a poem? Why might a poet want you to remember the words of his poem?

Do you think a cowboy's life is a good life? Would you like to be a cowboy?

THE COWBOY'S LIFE

The bawl of a steer,
To a cowboy's ear,
Is music of sweetest strain;
And the yelping notes
Of the gay coyotes
To him are a glad refrain.

For a kingly crown
In the noisy town
His saddle he wouldn't change;
No life so free
As the life we see
Way out on the Yaso range.

The rapid beat
Of his broncho's feet
On the sod as he speeds along,
Keeps living time
To the ringing rhyme
Of his rollicking cowboy song.

The winds may blow
And the thunder growl
Or the breezes may safely moan;—
A cowboy's life
Is a royal life,
His saddle his kingly throne.

—Attributed to
JAMES BARTON ADAMS

According to this poem, is the cowboy's life a good life? What words in the poem give you clues about his life? Do cowboys ever have unpleasant experiences? Why do you think the poet doesn't tell about those experiences?

What kind of sound does the rapid beat of a broncho's feet make? When you read this poem out loud, what does its rhythm sound like?

The last stanza of the poem says that the thunder may *growl* as the cowboy rides the range. If you say *growl* out loud, you'll notice that the word sounds something like a growl. What other words in the poem imitate the sounds they mean?

From the sounds, can you tell what is happening in this poem?

CAT!

Cat!
Scat!
After her, after her,
Sleeky flatterer,
Spitfire chatterer,
Scatter her, scatter her
Off her mat!
Wuff!
Wuff!
Treat her rough!
Git her, git her,
Whiskery spitter!
Catch her, catch her,
Green-eyed scratcher!
Slathery
Slithery
Hisser,
Don't miss her!
Run till you're dithery,
Hithery
Thithery
Pftts! pftts!
How she spits!

Spitch! Spatch!
Can't she scratch!
Scritching the bark
Of the sycamore-tree,
She's reached her ark
And's hissing at me
Pftts! pftts!
Wuff! wuff!
   Scat,
   Cat!
   That's
   That!

—ELEANOR FARJEON

What is happening in this poem? Who's chasing? Who's being chased? Who wins?

You could read this drama aloud, with one reader playing the part of the dog, and another reader playing the part of the cat. Which words imitate a dog? Which words imitate a cat? Who might be saying or thinking the rest of the poem: the dog, the cat, or someone watching the chase?

What letter sounds do you hear over and over again in the whole poem? How do the sounds fit what is happening?

You probably noticed that this poem is written in short lines. How does the length of the lines suggest the way the cat and the dog move?

What words can you think of or make up to imitate the sounds of jazz?

JAZZ FANTASIA

Drum on your drums, batter on your banjos, sob on the
    long cool winding saxophones. Go to it, O jazzmen.

Sling your knuckles on the bottoms of the happy tin
    pans, let your trombones ooze, and go husha-husha-
    hush with the slippery sandpaper.

Moan like an autumn wind high in the lonesome tree-
    tops, moan soft like you wanted somebody terrible,
    cry like a racing car slipping away from a motorcycle-
    cop, bang-bang! you jazzmen, bang altogether drums,
    traps, banjos, horns, tin cans—make two people fight
    on the top of a stairway and scratch each other's eyes
    in a clinch tumbling down the stairs.

Can the rough stuff . . . Now a Mississippi steamboat
    pushes up the night river with a hoo-hoo-hoo-oo
    . . . and the green lanterns calling to the high soft
    stars . . . a red moon rides on the humps of the low
    river hills. . . . Go to it, O jazzmen.

—CARL SANDBURG

What words did Carl Sandburg use to imitate the sounds jazz instruments make?

Why do you think the poet says "long cool winding" to describe the saxophone, rather than "long, cool, and winding"? What words does he use to describe the tin pans and the sandpaper?

How does the length of the third stanza suggest what is happening in the music? What scenes does the music suggest to Sandburg? What feelings belong to the scenes?

What scene does the last stanza describe? What feeling does the music end with?

From "Jazz Fantasia" can you tell what a *fantasia* is?

✸ ✸ ✸

Words Imitate Sounds

In the poems you have read, you have already found many words which imitate sounds. Which words were so vivid that you remember them without glancing back at the poems?

Sometimes a poet makes up a new word to imitate a special sound. Both "Cat!" and "Jazz Fantasia" contain words you can't find in the dictionary. Yet you could understand those words because they imitate familiar sounds.

Sit very still and listen. What sounds do you hear that you didn't notice a few minutes ago? What words will imitate the sounds you hear? Choose a noisy place, like a ball park, a farmyard, a carnival, the street in front of your house, or some other place. What words can you think of or make up to imitate the sounds of your chosen place? See if other people can guess what place you have chosen from your words.

✸ ✸ ✸

This chant was sung by the Osage Indians before a buffalo hunt. The Indians lived so close to nature that they could imagine themselves as buffaloes.

THE RISING OF THE BUFFALO MEN

I rise, I rise,
I, whose tread makes the earth to rumble.

I rise, I rise,
I, in whose thighs there is strength.

I rise, I rise,
I, who whips his back with his tail when in rage.

I rise, I rise,
I, in whose humped shoulder there is power.

I rise, I rise,
I, who shakes his mane when angered.

I rise, I rise,
I, whose horns are sharp and curved.
—AMERICAN INDIAN CHANT

The Indians often danced as they chanted. What movement might dancers make each time they repeat "I rise, I rise"? What movement might go with the second line of each stanza?

Notice that the song starts with the buffalo's feet (his "tread") and ends at his horns. How does this order of describing the parts of a buffalo fit with the line repeated in the song?

What impression of the buffalo does the song as a whole give? Do you think the Indians admired or feared the buffalo?

BUFFALO DUSK

The buffaloes are gone.
And those who saw the buffaloes are gone.
Those who saw the buffaloes by thousands and
    how they pawed the prairie sod into dust
    with their hoofs, their great heads down
    pawing on in a great pageant of dusk,
Those who saw the buffaloes are gone.
And the buffaloes are gone.

—CARL SANDBURG

Sometimes when you are very happy (or sad), one thought keeps coming into your mind, and it seems as if you can think of nothing else. What words keep coming back into this poem? What mood might cause this repetition?

Why do you think the poet made the third line longer than the other lines of the poem? What is a pageant? Why do you suppose Sandburg says "a great pageant of *dusk*" in the third line and titles the poem "Buffalo *Dusk*"?

Can people be happy without fine houses and possessions? How?

BRIAN O LINN

Brian O Linn had no breeches to wear,
He got an old sheepskin to make him a pair.
With the fleshy side out and the woolly side in,
"They'll be pleasant and cool," says Brian O Linn.

Brian O Linn had no shirt to his back,
He went to a neighbor's, and borrowed a sack,
Then he puckered the meal bag in under his chin—
"Sure they'll take them for ruffles," says Brian O Linn.

Brian O Linn was hard up for a coat,
So he borrowed the skin of a neighboring goat,
With the horns sticking out from his oxsters, and then,
"Sure they'll take them for pistols," says Brian O Linn.

Brian O Linn had no hat to put on,
So he got an old beaver to make him a one,
There was none of the crown left and less of the brim,
"Sure there's fine ventilation," says Brian O Linn.

Brian O Linn had no brogues for his toes,
He hopped in two crab-shells to serve him for those.
Then he split up two oysters that match'd like a twin,
"Sure they'll shine out like buckles," says Brian O Linn.

Brian O Linn had no watch to put on,
So he scooped out a turnip to make him a one.
Then he placed a young cricket in-under the skin—
"Sure they'll think it is ticking," says Brian O Linn.

Brian O Linn to his house had no door,
He'd the sky for a roof, and the bog for a floor;
He'd a way to jump out, and a way to swim in,
" 'Tis a fine habitation," says Brian O Linn.

—IRISH BALLAD

Which of Brian O Linn's substitutes seems the cleverest? Would
you like to live like Brian O Linn? Would he be a pleasant person
to know?

Which lines sound alike, although they aren't exact repeti-
tions? What words are repeated exactly? How is what happens
in each stanza a repetition?

✓ ✓ ✓

DREAMS

Hold fast to dreams
For if dreams die
Life is a broken-winged bird
That cannot fly.

Hold fast to dreams
For when dreams go
Life is a barren field
Frozen with snow.

—LANGSTON HUGHES

What kind of dreams do you think Langston Hughes is talking about? What does he advise you to do with dreams?

What does he say a life without dreams is like? What mood do the two comparisons suggest to you?

How are the two stanzas alike?

✦ ✦ ✦

Plains Indians faced many hardships on long marches across the prairies. In this chant a young warrior on the march speaks.

DRY IS MY TONGUE

Dry is my tongue from marching,
O, my elder brother, O, my elder brother.
Dry is my tongue from marching,
And, lo, death draws near to me.
Dry is my tongue from marching,
O, my elder brother, O, my elder brother.
Dry is my tongue from marching.

—AMERICAN INDIAN CHANT

What lines are repeated? Why do you think the young warrior keeps repeating them?

Do you think the young warrior gives up and dies, or keeps on marching? What hint does the repetition in the poem give?

✓ ✓ ✓

Repetition Emphasizes

Repetition can be either good or bad. It may be a waste of time, and it may be irritating, especially if the words repeat something you'd rather not hear in the first place—directions like "Clean up your room" or "Be sure to be home by nine o'clock."

But repetition can also be helpful. If someone is telling some unbelievable news, you may need to hear the words repeated before you are sure you heard correctly. And repetition can be enjoyable. In some songs, for instance, there is something comfortably familiar about repeated words. They keep running through your mind, and the more you hear them, the more you like them.

You probably remember several lines or phrases that were repeated in the poems you have just read. A poet often repeats on purpose, to help you remember. Sometimes, the second or third time you read repeated words, you discover a deeper meaning than you found the first time you read them.

Listen to people for the next twenty-four hours—at home, at school, on television, anywhere. Jot down some words they repeat. Why do you think they repeated the words? Were they trying to annoy or to help you? Were they trying to emphasize the idea so that you wouldn't forget it? Were they repeating in order to be humorous? Did you enjoy hearing the repeated words? Did the repetition, perhaps, add a new meaning to a statement? Or did the repetition have another purpose or effect? Was there just one reason or a combination of reasons?

✓ ✓ ✓

Have you ever eaten an eel? Would you like to?

THE EEL

I don't mind eels
Except as meals
And the way they feels.

—OGDEN NASH

What special sound effect holds the three lines of the poem together?

Is "they feels" good English? Why do you think the poet said it?

THE DUCK

Behold the duck.
It does not cluck.
A cluck it lacks.
It quacks.
It is specially fond
Of a puddle or pond.
When it dines or sups,
It bottoms ups.

—OGDEN NASH

16

If you were going on an ocean voyage, what kind of ship would you choose? How would you feel if the ship ran aground on a tropical island?

THE WALLOPING WINDOW-BLIND

A capital ship for an ocean trip
  Was *The Walloping Window-blind;*
No gale that blew dismayed her crew
  Or troubled the captain's mind.
The man at the wheel was taught to feel
  Contempt for the wildest blow,
And it often appeared, when the weather had cleared,
  That he'd been in his bunk below.

The boatswain's mate was very sedate,
  Yet fond of amusement, too;
And he played hop-scotch with the starboard watch
  While the captain tickled the crew.
And the gunner we had was apparently mad,
  For he sat on the after-rail,
And fired salutes with the captain's boots,
  In the teeth of the booming gale.

The captain sat in a commodore's hat,
  And dined, in a royal way,
On toasted pigs and pickles and figs
  And gummery bread, each day.

But the cook was Dutch, and behaved as such;
    For the food that he gave the crew
Was a number of tons of hot-cross buns,
    Chopped up with sugar and glue.

And we all felt ill as mariners will,
    On a diet that's cheap and rude;
And we shivered and shook as we dipped the cook
    In a tub of his gluesome food.
Then nautical pride we laid aside,
    And we cast the vessel ashore
On the Gulliby Isles, where the Poohpooh smiles,
    And the Anagazanders roar.

Composed of sand was that favored land,
    And trimmed with cinnamon straws;
And pink and blue was the pleasing hue
    Of the Tickletoeteaser's claws.
And we sat on the edge of a sandy ledge
    And shot at the whistling bee;
And the Binnacle-bats wore water-proof hats
    As they danced in the sounding sea.

On rubagub bark, from dawn to dark,
    We fed, till we all had grown
Uncommonly shrunk,—when a Chinese junk
    Came by from the torriby zone.

She was stubby and square, but we didn't much care,
   And we cheerily put to sea;
And we left the crew of the junk to chew
   The bark of the rubagub tree.

                             —CHARLES E. CARRYL

Would this ship qualify for your ocean voyage? Even if it wouldn't qualify, are there parts of the voyage that you might enjoy?

What kind of motion does the rhythm of this poem suggest? What kind of motion would you expect from a ship named "The Walloping Window-blind"?

What words do you notice in the poem that sound funny or delightful even if you aren't quite sure what they mean?

Which words inside lines rhyme with words at the ends of lines? What other rhymes do you find in each stanza?

What should a witch look like? What is she supposed to do?
Is the witch in this poem a usual or an unusual witch?

THE WITCH OF WILLOWBY WOOD

There once was a witch of Willowby Wood,
and a weird wild witch was she, with hair that was snarled
and hands that were gnarled, and a kickety, rickety
knee. She could jump, they say,
to the moon and back, but this I never did see.
Now Willowby Wood was near Sassafras Swamp,
where there's never a road or rut. And there by the
singing witch-hazel bush the old woman builded
her hut. She builded with neither a hammer or shovel. She
kneaded, she rolled out, she baked
her brown hovel. For *all* witches' houses, I've oft heard
it said, are made of stick candy and fresh
gingerbread. But the shingles that shingled this old
witch's roof were lollipop shingles and hurricane-proof, too
hard to be pelted and melted by rain.
(Why this is important, I soon will explain.)
One day there came running to Sassafras Swamp a dark little
shadowy mouse. He was noted for being a scoundrel
and scamp. And he gnawed at the old woman's house where the
doorpost was weak and the doorpost was worn.
And when the witch scolded, he laughed her to scorn.
And when the witch chased him, he felt quite delighted. She
never could catch him for she was nearsighted. And so,
though she quibbled, he gnawed and he nibbled.

The witch said, "I won't have my house
take a tumble. I'll search in my magical book for a spell
I can weave and a charm I can mumble to get you
away from this nook. It will be a good warning to other
bad mice, who won't earn their bread
but go stealing a slice."
"Your charms cannot hurt," said the mouse, looking pert.
Well, she looked in her book and she
waved her right arm, and she said the most magical
things. Till the mouse, feeling strange,
looked about in alarm, and found he was growing some
wings. He flapped and he fluttered the longer she muttered.
"And now, my fine fellow,
you'd best be aloof," said the witch as he floundered
around. "You can't stay on earth and you
can't gnaw my roof. It's lollipop-hard and it's
hurricane-proof. So you'd better take off
from the ground. If you are wise, stay in the skies."
Then in went the woman of Willowby Wood,
in to her hearthstone and cat.
There she put her old volume up high on the shelf, and
fanned her hot face with her hat. Then she said,
"That is *that!* I have just made a *bat!*"

—ROWENA BENNETT

How does this poem look different on the page from other
poems you have read? Is the Witch of Willowby Wood herself different from other witches?

Do you think the mouse deserved what happened to him? Do
you think the witch hurt him? What does a bat look like? Does

a bat's appearance make it seem that this story could really have happened?

Read the first five lines out loud. Why didn't your voice pause at the end of every line?

The first five lines work together to give a single idea: they tell you what the witch looked like and what she could do. Rhyme holds these lines together so quietly that you may not have noticed the rhymes at first. What are the rhyming words in the first five lines?

The separate sets of rhyming words in the rest of the poem divide it into groups of lines, each group telling one part of the story. What rhymes do you notice especially? What particular part of the story does that set of rhyming lines tell?

✓ ✓ ✓

JABBERWOCKY

'Twas brillig, and the slithy toves
    Did gyre and gimble in the wabe:
All mimsy were the borogoves,
    And the mome raths outgrabe.

"Beware the Jabberwock, my son!
    The jaws that bite, the claws that catch!
Beware the Jubjub bird, and shun
    The frumious Bandersnatch!"

He took his vorpal sword in hand:
    Long time the manxome foe he sought—
So rested he by the Tumtum tree,
    And stood awhile in thought.

And, as in uffish thought he stood,
　　The Jabberwock, with eyes of flame,
Came whiffling through the tulgey wood,
　　And burbled as it came!

One, two! One, two! And through and through
　　The vorpal blade went snicker-snack!
He left it dead, and with its head
　　He went galumphing back.

"And hast thou slain the Jabberwock?
　　Come to my arms, my beamish boy!
O frabjous day! Callooh! Callay!"
　　He chortled in his joy.

'Twas brillig, and the slithy toves
　　Did gyre and gimble in the wabe:
All mimsy were the borogoves,
　　And the mome raths outgrabe.

—LEWIS CARROLL

Here's a puzzle. "The Sniffle" may *look* strange the first time you read it, but it will make sense when you read it out loud. The sound of the rhymes is the secret. As you read, remember that Isabel has a sniffle. How do people with a cold sound when they say "I've got a cold in my nose"?

THE SNIFFLE

In spite of her sniffle,
Isabel's chiffle.
Some girls with a sniffle
Would be weepy and tiffle;
They would look awful,
Like a rained-on waffle,
But Isabel's chiffle
In spite of her sniffle.
Her nose is more red
With a cold in her head,
But then, to be sure,
Her eyes are bluer.
Some girls with a snuffle,
Their tempers are uffle,
But when Isabel's snivelly
She's snivelly civilly,
And when she's snuffly
She's perfectly luffly.

—OGDEN NASH

Rhyme Connects

In the poems you have just read, you have seen how lines, stanzas, and even entire poems are connected by rhyme. Some rhymes are funny or surprising; some are simply pleasing in a quiet way. Sometimes you notice them immediately; sometimes you have to look for them.

Rhyme often makes it easier to remember words and their meanings. For example, what poem does the following sentence remind you of?

I do not object to snake-like water animals, unless they
are served for dinner, or unless I have to touch them.

Which is easier to remember: the sentence or the poem?

Advertisers have caught on to the uses of rhyme. They frequently use jingles to get you to remember and buy their products. In everyday talk, too, people sometimes rhyme words, often without intending to. Listen for an interesting spoken rhyme to share with the class. Be ready to tell where you heard the rhyme and whether you think it was made up for a purpose or just happened by chance.

✓ ✓ ✓

Most bats sleep during the day. But in a story by Randall Jarrell, one bat was so pleased by a mockingbird's songs that he decided to write poems himself. To observe the daytime animals he wanted to write about, he had to open his eyes, even though the sunlight hurt. Here is the poem he wrote about his friend, the chipmunk.

THE CHIPMUNK'S DAY

In and out the bushes, up the ivy,
Into the hole
By the old oak stump, the chipmunk flashes.
Up the pole

To the feeder full of seeds he dashes,
Stuffs his cheeks,
The chickadee and titmouse scold him.
Down he streaks.

Red as the leaves the wind blows off the maple,
Red as a fox,
Striped like a skunk, the chipmunk whistles
Past the love seat, past the mailbox,

Down the path,
Home to his warm hole stuffed with sweet
Things to eat.
Neat and slight and shining, his front feet

Curled at his breast, he sits there while the sun
Stripes the red west
With its last light: the chipmunk
Dives to his rest.

—RANDALL JARRELL

What does the chipmunk do during the day? Find the verbs which tell how he moves. Which one imitates a sound he makes? Why do you think the poet used so many different verbs?

In the story, the chipmunk is very pleased with the verse portrait of him that the bat has written. "Oh, it's nice," he says. "It all goes in and out, doesn't it?" Look at the lines in the poem. How do they go "in and out"? Why would the chipmunk like having the poem go in and out?

What punctuation marks do you find at the ends of stanzas? What does this punctuation suggest you should do when you read the poem aloud? How does the way you read fit the way the chipmunk moves?

Several patterns of sound help the words in this poem fit together. For instance, what word combinations start with the same first letter?

Which lines rhyme in each stanza? Is the rhyme pattern exactly the same for each stanza? Does any line in one stanza rhyme with a line in another stanza? Why wouldn't a pattern of rhymes like the one in "The Walloping Window-blind" suit the description of the chipmunk's day?

In Shakespeare's play *The Tempest*, the survivors of a shipwreck are cast ashore on a magic island. Ariel, a friendly spirit of the island, sings this song to Ferdinand, Prince of Naples, to tell him what has happened to his father.

FULL FATHOM FIVE

Full fathom five thy father lies:
   Of his bones are coral made;
Those are pearls that were his eyes;
   Nothing of him that doth fade
But doth suffer a sea-change
Into something rich and strange.
Sea-nymphs hourly ring his knell:
                Ding-dong!
Hark! now I hear them,—Ding-dong, bell!

—WILLIAM SHAKESPEARE

According to Ariel, what has happened to the King of Naples? If you were drawing a picture to illustrate the song, would it be a beautiful or ugly picture? Would black and white or color be more appropriate? What words or details in the poem suggest what kind of picture it would be?

The first line of this song is held together by an interesting sound effect. What repeated sounds do you notice especially? The first line also uses an unusual word order. Say the words in the order we would ordinarily put them, starting with "Thy father." What is the difference in emphasis and effect between the ordinary spoken way and the way the poem was written?

A *knell* is a slow, solemn bell rung to announce a death. What words imitate the sound of this particular knell? Do these words sound sad when you say them by themselves? How does the poet use rhyme to make you notice these words especially?

(NOTE: You may be happy to know that Ferdinand's father wasn't drowned after all. He and his followers had been cast ashore on the same island, but in a different spot.)

A chantey was a song which sailors on the old sailing vessels sang as they worked. The song helped them pull the ropes in rhythm as they heaved the anchor or hoisted sail.

THE SEA SERPENT CHANTEY

I

There's a snake on the western wave
And his crest is red.
He is long as a city street,
And he eats the dead.
There's a hole in the bottom of the sea
Where the snake goes down.
And he waits in the bottom of the sea
For the men that drown.

CHORUS:
This is the voice of the sand
(The sailors understand)
"There is far more sea than sand,
There is far more sea than land.
    Yo . . . ho, yo . . . ho."

*Let the
audience
join in
the chorus.*

II

He waits by the door of his cave
While the ages moan.
He cracks the ribs of the ships
With his teeth of stone.
In his gizzard deep and long
Much treasure lies.
Oh, the pearls and the Spanish gold . . .
And the idols' eyes . . .

Oh, the totem poles . . . the skulls . . .
The altars cold . . .
The wedding rings, the dice . . .
The buoy bells old.
   CHORUS: This is the voice, etc.

III

Dive, mermaids, with sharp swords
And cut him through,
And bring us the idols' eyes
And the red gold too.
Lower the grappling hooks
Good pirate men
And drag him up by the tongue
From his deep wet den.
We will sail to the end of the world,   *Repeat as a*
We will nail his hide   *second chorus*
To the mainmast of the moon   *many times.*
In the evening tide.

IV

Or will you let him live,
The deep-sea thing,
With the wrecks of all the world
In a black wide ring
By the hole in the bottom of the sea
Where the snake goes down,
Where he waits in the bottom of the sea
For the men that drown?
    CHORUS: This is the voice, etc.

—VACHEL LINDSAY

Which of the sea serpent's treasures would you most like to see? Which would you rather have the mermaids do—cut the serpent through or let him live?

Sailors didn't actually sing this particular chantey. A modern poet wrote it as an imitation of the old-time chanteys. Why do you think he chose a sea serpent to be the subject of his poem?

Does it make any difference whether the statements in the poem are really so? Do you think everything in a poem has to be true to fact to say something true or important?

On which words in the first stanza might the sailors all pull together? On which words in the chorus? To find these words, try reading the poem aloud, making motions as if you were pulling on a rope.

What other patterns of sound besides rhythm help the words in this poem fit together?

How does a cat walk in a narrow place, such as along the top
of a fence?

POEM

As the cat
climbed over
the top of

the jamcloset
first the right
forefoot

carefully
then the hind
stepped down

into the pit of
the empty
flowerpot

—**WILLIAM CARLOS WILLIAMS**

What word in the poem sums up the way the cat moves?

Read the first stanza aloud. Does it read smoothly or jerkily?
How do you picture the cat to be moving at the beginning of
the poem?

The words "of the jamcloset" would ordinarily be written together. Why do you think they are separated by a stanza division?
What might the cat be doing at this point?

As you read the rest of the poem aloud, how long will you want
to pause at the end of each line? How long should your pauses at
the end of each stanza probably be? How will your pauses suggest
the way the cat is moving?

Picture in your mind the cat's position at the end of the poem.
Why you suppose the poem doesn't stop with a period, even at
the end? What do you think the cat will do next?

Can you find any rhyme in this poem? Does a poem *have* to
rhyme?

Why do you think Mr. Williams called his description of the
cat "Poem"?

n
OthI
n

g can

s
urPas
s

the m

y
SteR
y
of
s
tilLnes
s

—E. E. CUMMINGS

Did this poem look strange to you at first? In what ways does
it look different from other poems you've read? Say the poem
as an ordinary sentence. Why do you think the poet made the poem
the way he did? Why do you suppose he didn't give the poem
a title?

Which stanzas have the same shape on the page? What design or pattern can you see in the way the stanzas occur?

Try reading this poem aloud. How should the letters which have whole lines to themselves sound? Consider, too, whether the capital letters should be pronounced differently from the other letters. After the reading, what sounds are left in your ears? Are they sounds that seem to fit the mood of this poem?

✓ ✓ ✓

A Poet's Ears

A poet's ears are tuned in clearly to the sound of words. You may be wondering if he thinks, when he writes, about all the many ways of using sound. Perhaps not. Sometimes a poem comes to him easily, and the words just sound right or feel right.

But many poets make dozens of pages of revisions, all of the same short poem. When the poet is dissatisfied with the words in his poem, he experiments with sound and meaning together.

A poet who writes regularly is studying the anatomy of sounds just as a physician studies the anatomy of the human body. A poem by a good poet is like the dance of a good ballet dancer, or like the pivot of a professional basketball player. Their movements look easy, effortless. The dancer moves as if all she has to do is float along with the music. The basketball player moves as if all he has to do is turn around. But have you ever tried to imitate the ballerina or the pro? Why couldn't you do it, at least at first?

2

POEMS
TELL
STORIES

AT MEALS, people often talk about what has happened during the day. Newspapers report events of yesterday. Stories in literature tell of imaginary experiences of the past, of the present, or even of the future.

All three—table conversation, newspaper reports, and imagined stories—interest people for the same reason. We all want to know what has happened and is happening in the world around us. We all wonder what the future will be.

Imagined stories are especially satisfying. In them you can read about the past, the present, and sometimes the future of people or animals who interest you. The characters interest you partly because the author helps you know them well enough to understand them. How might you explain the other reasons for your interest in imaginary characters?

Not all stories cover an entire lifetime of an imagined character. Sometimes they tell of only a single event. In life, you may meet a person just once, and yet you remember the meeting forever. What would cause you to remember? Why might an author choose to tell only one event in the life of an imaginary character, rather than about his entire life?

Stories told in verse are especially memorable. The sounds of the words help you remember the characters and their adventures. Many of the very earliest English poems that have lived until today tell stories.

The earliest poems were spoken, rather than written. It is only by lucky accident that we have some of them written down. Some of the story poems were first composed by wandering poets called minstrels.

It was natural for the minstrel, as he wandered from castle to castle, to chant his stories, sometimes to music. As he told and re-told the stories, he would leave out unimportant details and connect the sounds of the words more smoothly. His stories, often about current events, became polished poems. People listened to them over and over again for pleasure, rather than just for information.

Not all stories told in poems are as old as the minstrels' songs. Recognizing that everyone enjoys a story, modern poets, too, have often chosen to write story poems. Often the people or animals they write about seem very like the characters in the minstrels' songs.

The catbird's name comes from one of its songs, which sounds like mewing. All its other songs, too, are only imitations. How do you think a catbird might feel about not having a real song of its own?

THE KITTY-CAT BIRD

The Kitty-Cat Bird, he sat on a Fence.
Said the Wren, your Song isn't worth 10¢.
You're a Fake, you're a Fraud, you're a Hor-rid
    Pretense!
    —Said the Wren to the Kitty-Cat Bird.

You've too many Tunes, and none of them Good:
I wish you would act like a bird really should,
Or stay by yourself down deep in the wood,
    —Said the Wren to the Kitty-Cat Bird.

You mew like a Cat, you grate like a Jay:
You squeak like a Mouse that's lost in the Hay,
I wouldn't be You for even a day,
    —Said the Wren to the Kitty-Cat Bird.

The Kitty-Cat Bird, he moped and he cried.
Then a real cat came with a Mouth so Wide,
That the Kitty-Cat Bird just hopped inside;
"At last I'm myself!"—and he up and died
    —Did the Kitty—the Kitty-Cat Bird.

You'd better not laugh; and don't say "Pooh!"
Until you have thought this Sad Tale through:
Be sure that whatever you are is you
    —Or you'll end like the Kitty-Cat Bird.
                        —THEODORE ROETHKE

What did the Wren think of the Kitty-Cat Bird? What words imitate the catbird's songs? Which of the Wren's comments seems the most unkind? Why did the Kitty-Cat Bird react as he did?

Some poems may sound childish at first, but when you think about them, you find they express important ideas. Why do you think Roethke called the catbird the "Kitty-Cat Bird" in this poem?

In ancient Greece, a man named Aesop wrote some very short stories called fables. In Aesop's fables, animals talk and act like human beings. At the end of each fable, a moral states the story's lesson about how people should act. What is the moral of the modern fable "The Kitty-Cat Bird"? Do you think the moral is true?

Have you ever seen a flying fish? If not, can you imagine what one must look like? Why might it be easy to think of flattering things to say to a flying fish?

THE FLATTERED FLYING FISH

Said the Shark to the Flying Fish over the phone:
'Will you join me tonight? I am dining alone.
Let me order a nice little dinner for two!
And come as you are, in your shimmering blue.'

Said the Flying Fish: 'Fancy remembering me,
And the dress that I wore at the Porpoises' tea!'
'How could I forget?' said the Shark in his guile:
'I expect you at eight!' and rang off with a smile.

She has powdered her nose; she has put on her things;
She is off with one flap of her luminous wings.
O little one, lovely, light-hearted and vain,
The Moon will not shine on your beauty again!

—E. V. RIEU

What words in the poem help you to see the Flying Fish? How did the Shark flatter her? How does the story help you discover the meaning of *guile?*

In the last two lines, the poet speaks directly to the Flying Fish. Do you think he likes the Flying Fish? What does he think of her character? What does he predict will happen to her? Do you think he is right?

How do the Shark and the Flying Fish remind you of people?

You will follow the next story more easily if you listen for the voices of its main characters. The cockroach, archy, tells the story. In his story three other characters speak: (1) the stranger, a tough-looking tarantula with a lot of legs, (2) the local creature called "thousand legs," and (3) freddy the rat, the hero of the story. The scene is a newspaper office after working hours when all the insects and rodents come out of hiding.

freddy the rat perishes

listen to me there have
been some doings here since last
i wrote there has been a battle
behind that rusty typewriter cover
in the corner
you remember freddy the rat well
freddy is no more but
he died game the other
day a stranger with a lot of
legs came into our
little circle a tough looking kid
he was with a bad eye
who are you said a thousand legs

if i bite you once
said the stranger you won't ask
again he he little poison tongue said
the thousand legs who gave you hydrophobia
i got it by biting myself said
the stranger i'm bad keep away
from me where i step a weed dies
if i was to walk on your forehead it would
raise measles and if
you give me any lip i ll do it
they mixed it then
and the thousand legs succumbed
well we found out this fellow
was a tarantula he had come up from
south america in a bunch of bananas
for days he bossed us life
was not worth living he would stand in
the middle of the floor and taunt
us ha ha he would say where i
step a weed dies do
you want any of my game i was
raised on red pepper and blood i am
so hot if you scratch me i will light
like a match you better
dodge me when i m feeling mean and
i don t feel any other way i was nursed
on a tabasco bottle if i was to slap
your wrist in kindness you
would boil over like job and heaven
help you if i get angry give me
room i feel a wicked spell coming on

last night he made a break at freddy
the rat keep your distance
little one said freddy i m not
feeling well myself somebody poisoned some
cheese for me i m as full of
death as a drug store i
feel that i am going to die anyhow
come on little torpedo come on don t stop
to visit and search then they
went at it and both are no more please
throw a late edition on the floor i want to
keep up with china we dropped freddy
off the fire escape into the alley with
military honors

—archy
(DON MARQUIS)

It will help you hear how the stranger and the thousand legs started fighting if you read the part of thousand legs aloud in one tone of voice and the part of the stranger (the tarantula) in another voice. Read freddy's words in still a different tone of voice.

What effect did the tarantula have on everyone else? Which of his taunts sounds the most menacing?

Why did freddy fight? Why did the others drop freddy off the fire escape with military honors?

Are you wondering why there are no capital letters in this poem? Don Marquis, a journalist, claimed that his poems were batted out on his typewriter at night by a cockroach named archy, who couldn't jump on both the shift key and a letter key at the same time to make a capital letter.

In the days when Ireland was ruled by England, Irish boys were often enlisted to fight for England in foreign wars.

MRS. McGRATH

"Oh Mrs. McGrath!" the sergeant said,
"Would you like to make a soldier out of your son, Ted,
With a scarlet coat and a big cocked hat,
Now Mrs. McGrath, wouldn't you like that?"
> CHORUS:
> Wid yer too-ri-aa, fol-the-diddle-aa
> Too-ri-oo-ri-oo-ri-aa,
> Wid your too-ri-aa Fol-the-diddle-aa
> Too-ri-oo-ri-oo-ri-aa.

So Mrs. McGrath lived on the sea-shore
For the space of seven long years or more
Till she saw a big ship sailing into the bay
"Here's my son Ted, wisha, clear the way."   (CHORUS)

"Oh, Captain dear, where have you been?
Have you been sailing on the Mediterreen?
Or have ye any tidings of my son Ted?
Is the poor boy living or is he dead?"   (CHORUS)

Then up comes Ted without any legs
And in their place he has two wooden pegs.
She kissed him a dozen times or two
Saying "Holy Moses 'tisn't you."   (CHORUS)

"Oh then were ye drunk or were ye blind
That ye left yer two fine legs behind?
Or was it walking upon the sea
Wore yer two fine legs from the knees away?"   (CHORUS)

"Oh I wasn't drunk and I wasn't blind,
But I left my two fine legs behind.
For a cannon ball on the fifth of May
Took my two fine legs from the knees away."   (CHORUS)

"Oh then Teddy me boy," the widow cried,
"Yer two fine legs were yer mammy's pride!
Them stumps of a tree wouldn't do at all.
Why didn't ye run from the big cannon ball?   (CHORUS)

All foreign wars I do proclaim
Between Don John and the King of Spain,
And by herrins I'll make them rue the time
That they swept the legs from a child of mine. (CHORUS)

Oh then, if I had you back again
I'd never let ye go to fight the King of Spain
For I'd rather my Ted as he used to be
Than the King of France and his whole Navee."

(CHORUS)
—IRISH BALLAD

How does a soldier's life sound in the first stanza? In the third
and fourth stanzas?

In stanza five, Mrs. McGrath sounds as if she is scolding her
son for losing his legs. But where do you learn her true feelings?
What or whom does she *really* blame for her son's being disabled?

The chorus of "Mrs. McGrath" is composed of syllables rather
than words. However, these syllables may have been formed from
real words of an earlier version of the song. How could a singer
vary the way he sings the chorus to fit the mood of each stanza?

Where are men being replaced by machines today? In the 1870's automation threatened men who were carving railway tunnels out of the mountains in West Virginia. John Henry decided to race the steam drill to prove which was stronger: a man or a machine.

JOHN HENRY

When John Henry was a little baby,
Sitting on his papa's knee,
Well he picked up a hammer and a little piece of steel,
Said, "Hammer's gonna be the death of me, Lord, Lord!
Hammer's gonna be the death of me."

The captain said to John Henry,
"I'm gonna bring that steam drill around,
I'm gonna bring that steam drill out on the job,
I'm gonna whup that steel on down, Lord, Lord!
Whup that steel on down."

John Henry told his captain,
"Lord a man ain't nothing but a man,
But before I'd let your steam drill beat me down,
I'd die with a hammer in my hand, Lord, Lord!
Die with a hammer in my hand."

John Henry said to his shaker,
"Shaker why don't you sing?
Because I'm swinging thirty pounds from my hips on
    down;
Just listen to that cold steel ring, Lord, Lord!
Listen to that cold steel ring."

Now the captain said to John Henry,
"I believe that mountain's caving in."
John Henry said right back to the captain,
"Ain't nothing but my hammer catching wind, Lord,
    Lord!
Nothing but my hammer catching wind."

Now the man that invented the steam drill,
He thought he was mighty fine;
But John Henry drove fifteen feet,
The steam drill only made nine, Lord, Lord!
Steam drill only made nine.

John Henry hammered in the mountains,
His hammer was striking fire,
But he worked so hard it broke his poor heart
And he laid down his hammer and he died, Lord, Lord!
Laid down his hammer and he died.

Now John Henry had a little woman,
Her name was Polly Anne,
John Henry took sick and had to go to bed,
Polly Anne drove steel like a man, Lord, Lord!
Polly Anne drove steel like a man.

John Henry had a little baby,
You could hold him in the palm of your hand;
And the last words I heard that poor boy say,
"My daddy was a steel driving man, Lord, Lord!
My daddy was a steel driving man."

So every Monday morning
When the blue birds begin to sing,
You can hear John Henry a mile or more;
You can hear John Henry's hammer ring, Lord, Lord!
Hear John Henry's hammer ring.

—AMERICAN BALLAD

A steel-driving man like John Henry would drive a six-foot drill into the mountain side with steady hammer strokes while his shaker would twist the drill a quarter turn each time the driver struck it. Afterwards, other men would clear the tunnel of shattered rock.

Why does John Henry decide to race? Who really wins the race: the man or the machine? What differences between a man and a machine does the ballad show?

There are various versions of this story, but almost all versions include the opening scene of John Henry as a baby. How would the song be different if it left that scene out? Why are John Henry's Polly Anne and his baby mentioned at the end of the song?

How could John Henry's hammer be heard every Monday morning?

A Word About Ballads

The poems "Brian O Linn," "Mrs. McGrath," and "John Henry" are all the words to traditional songs, known as ballads. Perhaps many of these songs have lasted because they are about interesting characters. People may change the way they dress and eat and play over the years, but their important feelings don't change. For instance, do parents still feel the way Mrs. McGrath feels about her Ted?

Older ballads like "Mrs. McGrath" and "Brian O Linn" were passed down to us today orally, rather than in writing. A father would teach the songs to his son, and the son in turn would teach them to *his* son. Sometimes mothers and daughters were the singers. Over a period of time, singers might forget some words and make up new ones to fit the story and the rhythm of the words. Sometimes they would forget complete stanzas. The words to many ballads have been written down only recently. Some are still being discovered and recorded.

The process by which a ballad changes over the years is similar to what happens in the game of telephone, where the first person whispers a message to the next person, and so on down the line. The game is fun because the message is usually very different when it reaches the last person. Sometimes in the game you can trace where changes came in.

"John Henry" is based on an historical event of only a hundred years ago, but already it has many different versions because it has been sung so widely by so many singers. It's difficult, perhaps impossible, to know which version came first. Why do you suppose "John Henry" has been so popular?

A saltmarsh is a meadow covered with brackish water from the sea. In this desolate spot a nymph (in mythology a beautiful maiden dwelling in a mountain, forest, meadow, or waters) argues with a goblin (an ugly sprite, who could be either evil or playful).

OVERHEARD ON A SALTMARSH

Nymph, nymph, what are your beads?

Green glass, goblin. Why do you stare at them?

Give them me.

    No.

Give them me. Give them me.

    No.

Then I will howl all night in the reeds,
Lie in the mud and howl for them.

Goblin, why do you love them so?

They are better than stars or water,
Better than voices of winds that sing,
Better than any man's fair daughter,
Your green glass beads on a silver ring.

Hush, I stole them out of the moon.

Give me your beads, I want them.

No.

I will howl in a deep lagoon
For your green glass beads, I love them so.
Give them me. Give them.

No.

—HAROLD MONRO

Was the goblin evil or playful? What is special about the nymph's beads? Why does the goblin want them?

Why do you think the nymph wouldn't give her beads to the goblin?

What mood is created by the place, the characters, and their dialogue?

Nasturtium is the botanical name for both watercress and the common garden-variety flower you may know. Both plants grow very rapidly. The nasturtiums in this poem are an imaginary variety, but they are related in important ways to the real kinds.

THE BIG NASTURTIUMS

All of a sudden the big nasturtiums
Rose in the night from the ocean's bed,
Rested a while in the light of the morning,
Turning the sand dunes tiger red.

They covered the statue of Abraham Lincoln,
They climbed to the top of our church's spire.
"Grandpa! Grandpa! Come to the window!
Come to the window! Our world's on fire!"

Big nasturtiums in the High Sierras,
Big nasturtiums in the lands below;
Our trains are late and our planes have fallen,
And out in the ocean the whistles blow.

Over the fields and over the forests,
Over the living and over the dead—
"I never expected the big nasturtiums
To come in my lifetime!" Grandpa said.

—ROBERT BEVERLY HALE

It's clear what arose one night (in the poet's imagination) to take over the world. Why do you think the poet says the nasturtiums covered both the statue of Abraham Lincoln and the church's spire? What ideas do Lincoln and the church each stand for?

How does the poet imply that these nasturtiums are destructive? For example, why does the poet describe the color of the nasturtiums as *tiger* red? Why did the boy think the world was on fire?

Why do you suppose Grandpa was surprised that the big nasturtiums came in his lifetime? Do you think he may have expected them to come sometime after he was dead?

Why do you think the poet chose flowers as the agents of destruction? Did the destruction come from nature or from man? What might happen next?

✓ ✓ ✓

Have you ever heard music which seemed just right for that particular time? How did the music make you feel?

FIRST SONG

Then it was dusk in Illinois, the small boy
After an afternoon of carting dung
Hung on the rail fence, a sapped thing
Weary to crying. Dark was growing tall
And he began to hear the pond frogs all
Calling on his ear with what seemed their joy.

Soon their sound was pleasant for a boy
Listening in the smoky dusk and the nightfall
Of Illinois, and from the fields two small
Boys came bearing cornstalk violins
And they rubbed the cornstalk bows with resins
And the three sat there scraping of their joy.

It was now fine music the frogs and the boys
Did in the towering Illinois twilight make
And into dark in spite of a shoulder's ache
A boy's hunched body loved out of a stalk
The first song of his happiness, and the song woke
His heart to the darkness and into the sadness of joy.

—GALWAY KINNELL

53

What kind of music did the small boy hear? Why was it just right for the time he heard it?

How does the poet tell you in special ways that the boy was tired?

How do frogs sound at twilight? Can you imagine why the frogs sounded joyful to the boy?

What is the difference between saying, "It was getting dark," and "Dark was growing tall"? How does dark grow tall as night comes? How would a "smoky dusk" look?

Have you ever heard a cornstalk violin? What word in the second stanza gives you a clue to the kind of music the cornstalk violins made?

Why does the poet title this poem "First Song"—do you think the boy had never heard music before? How were joy and sadness mixed for the boy as he listened after an afternoon of hard work?

✶ ✶ ✶

When you look back on your childhood, can you remember imagining that you were both driving a car and *were* the car moving? Can you remember any other things you imagined yourself to be?

THE CENTAUR

The summer that I was ten—
Can it be there was only one
summer that I was ten? It must

have been a long one then—
each day I'd go out to choose
a fresh horse from my stable

which was a willow grove
down by the old canal.
I'd go on my two bare feet.

But when, with my brother's jack-knife,
I had cut me a long limber horse
with a good thick knob for a head,

and peeled him slick and clean
except a few leaves for the tail,
and cinched my brother's belt

around his head for a rein,
I'd straddle and canter him fast
up the grass bank to the path,

trot along in the lovely dust
that talcumed over his hoofs,
hiding my toes, and turning

his feet to swift half-moons.
The willow knob with the strap
jouncing between my thighs

was the pommel and yet the poll
of my nickering pony's head.
My head and my neck were mine,

yet they were shaped like a horse.
My hair flopped to the side
like the mane of a horse in the wind.

My forelock swung in my eyes,
my neck arched and I snorted.
I shied and skittered and reared,

stopped and raised my knees,
pawed at the ground and quivered.
My teeth bared as we wheeled

and swished through the dust again.
I was the horse and the rider,
and the leather I slapped to his rump

spanked my own behind.
Doubled, my two hoofs beat
a gallop along the bank,

the wind twanged in my mane,
my mouth squared to the bit.
And yet I sat on my steed

quiet, negligent riding,
my toes standing the stirrups,
my thighs hugging his ribs.

At a walk we drew up to the porch.
I tethered him to a paling.
Dismounting, I smoothed my skirt

and entered the dusky hall.
My feet on the clean linoleum
left ghostly toes in the hall.

Where have you been? said my mother.
Been riding, I said from the sink,
and filled me a glass of water.

What's that in your pocket? she said.
Just my knife. It weighted my pocket
and stretched my dress awry.

Go tie back your hair, said my mother,
and *Why is your mouth all green?*
*Rob Roy, he pulled some clover
as we crossed the field,* I told her.

—MAY SWENSON

Why do you think the speaker in this poem says that the summer was such a long one?

What did she do to the willow branch to turn it into a horse? How did her feet look when the dust hid her toes?

In Greek mythology, centaurs were men with the bodies of horses. In what ways, besides what happened to her feet, does the girl describe herself as both the horse and the rider? What words imitate the sounds a rider and a horse would make?

Why are the prints of her toes "ghostly" in the hall after she has dismounted? How does her mother treat her when she comes in? Why does the girl say what she says to explain why her mouth is green?

3

POEMS
DESCRIBE

THE SHUTTER of a high-speed camera opens for a fraction of a second. The eye of the camera catches a playful pet or a shy wild animal. If the photographer has been skillful and lucky, his picture will show the personality of the animal.

Perhaps the camera freezes a runner in one position, mouth gasping for air, arms hugging his sides, legs high. When you look at the picture, he almost seems to go on running, feet hitting the cinders. But for the moment captured in the picture, the runner is no longer earthbound.

Sometimes people agree to be photographed. Then the photographer can compose his portrait. He can decide whether his subject should sit or stand. He can arrange a background and adjust the shutter speed. With such elaborate preparation, the details of the portrait are sure to be distinct.

But distinctness alone does not make a good portrait. By this time, the sitter is probably tense. The picture will look stiff, posed. The photographer now has to use all his skill to help his subject relax. He wants the portrait to look natural, as though the sitter has just looked up from what he was doing.

Photographing a scene in nature may seem to be an easier task. Since trees and lakes and mountains don't move around, the photographer has more time to compose his picture. He can decide how to frame it and how to avoid any disrupting elements such as telephone wires.

But pictures of landscapes can be more interesting if there is life in them. A deer among the trees, the wind rippling a lake, a sunset glow on a mountain—these all add drama to a still scene. Because something interesting is happening, the scene will have meaning.

A poet, like a photographer. makes pictures of animals, people, and scenes. The poet uses words rather than film, but his method and purpose are much like those of a good photographer. Like a still photographer, the poet may pose his subject, or may catch his subject unaware at a characteristic moment. Like a movie cameraman, the poet may show his subject moving, talking, or changing over a period of time. Through his descriptions of animals, people, and scenes, the poet can help you find meaning in the living world about you.

Animals

Animal-watching is an interesting sport. Zoologists make a lifetime work of it. People often write complete books about their observations of one kind of animal, or even of a single animal.

A book about a raccoon, for example, will tell you all about his appearance, eating habits, habitat, and so on. The author may even comment on the raccoon's personality, as it appears to him.

When a poet writes about an animal, he picks out just one thing, or a few striking things, to tell you. He lets your knowledge or imagination fill in other details. The animal comes alive as you imagine the animal.

It would be interesting to hear a raccoon's comments on his own life, if animals and people could speak the same language. But for now, you can understand animals only through your own observations or those of other people such as zoologists and poets.

Why do you suppose zoologists, poets, and readers are all fascinated by animals?

What kind of pet would you most like to have? What would you name him?

STORMY

what name could
better
explode from

a sleeping pup
but this
leaping

to his feet
Stormy!
Stormy! Stormy!

—WILLIAM CARLOS WILLIAMS

(NOTE: Stormy was the name of the Williamses' Shetland sheep-dog.)

Why did the Williamses name their pet "Stormy"? How can a name "explode" from a pup?

What is Stormy doing at the beginning of the poem? Does the beginning sound quiet or excited?

What do you think Stormy is doing at the end of the poem? What makes you think so?

How do cats move, in comparison to dogs?

CATALOG

Cats sleep fat and walk thin.
Cats, when they sleep, slump;
When they wake, pull in —
And where the plump's been
There's skin.
Cats walk thin.

Cats wait in a lump,
Jump in a streak.
Cats, when they jump, are sleek
As a grape slipping its skin —
They have technique.
Oh, cats don't creak.
They sneak.

Cats sleep fat.
They spread comfort beneath them
Like a good mat,
As if they picked the place
And then sat.
You walk around one
As if he were the City Hall
After that.

If male,
A cat is apt to sing on a major scale;
This concert is for everybody, this
Is wholesale.
For a baton, he wields a tail.

(He is also found,
When happy, to resound
With an enclosed and private sound.)

A cat condenses.
He pulls in his tail to go under bridges,
And himself to go under fences.
Cats fit
In any size box or kit;
And if a large pumpkin grew under one,
He could arch over it.

When everyone else is just ready to go out,
The cat is just ready to come in.
He's not where he's been.
Cats sleep fat and walk thin.

—ROSALIE MOORE

What words in the poem seem especially appropriate to describe how cats sleep and move?

What is the way cats jump compared to? Why is it an appropriate comparison? What other comparisons can you find in the poem? How does each one fit the way a cat acts?

How is the fifth stanza different from the other stanzas? How do the differences fit the cat's actions in that stanza?

What other kinds of catalogs do you know? How are they similar? Why do you suppose Rosalie Moore called her poem "Catalog"?

Have you ever been frightened by a bat? Why are some people afraid of bats?

THE BAT

By day the bat is cousin to the mouse.
He likes the attic of an aging house.

His fingers make a hat about his head.
His pulse beat is so slow we think him dead.

He loops in crazy figures half the night
Among the trees that face the corner light.

But when he brushes up against a screen,
We are afraid of what our eyes have seen:

For something is amiss or out of place
When mice with wings can wear a human face.

—THEODORE ROETHKE

If you've never seen a bat close up (either because you've never been around bats or because you were too busy running from them) look at a picture of a bat. Is Roethke's description an accurate one?

Does the bat in the poem seem very frightening to you? Is he really likely to harm humans?

In the story *The Bat-Poet*, the bat made up a poem about the owl and then said it to the chipmunk, to show him what a portrait in verse was like.

THE BIRD OF NIGHT

A shadow is floating through the moonlight.
Its wings don't make a sound.
Its claws are long, its beak is bright.
Its eyes try all the corners of the night.

It calls and calls: all the air swells and heaves
And washes up and down like water.
The ear that listens to the owl believes
In death. The bat beneath the eaves,

The mouse beside the stone are still as death —
The owl's air washes them like water.
The owl goes back and forth inside the night,
And the night holds its breath.

—RANDALL JARRELL

Although he liked this poem, the chipmunk said it made him shiver. Why do you think he shivered at the poem about the owl? What is the owl doing at night? What feeling would make air seem to wash around animals like water?

Do people, like the chipmunk, sometimes enjoy shivering?

In some ancient countries, no one was allowed to look directly at the ruler. People could approach the king only while crawling on their knees or bowing double. Why do you suppose rulers made such rules?

LION

The lion, ruler over all the beasts,
Triumphant moves upon the grassy plain
With sun like gold upon his tawny brow
And dew like silver on his shaggy mane.

Into himself he draws the rolling thunder,
Beneath his flinty paw great boulders quake;
He will dispatch the mouse to burrow under,
The little deer to shiver in the brake.

He sets the fierce whip of each serpent lashing,
The tall giraffe brings humbly to his knees,
Awakes the sloth, and sends the wild boar crashing,
Wide-eyed monkeys chittering, through the trees.

He gazes down into the quiet river,
Parting the green bulrushes to behold
A sunflower-crown of amethyst and silver,
A royal coat of brushed and beaten gold.

—WILLIAM JAY SMITH

What kind of ruler is this lion? What would you do if you happened to meet him?

In the first stanza, how is the lion moving? Which lines in this stanza run into the following lines without pauses? Why do you think the poet ran these lines together?

What would a drawing of thunder "into himself" sound like? What domestic animal, related to the lion, makes a similar but smaller sound?

What is flint? Why does the poet call the lion's paw *flinty?*

How does the lion affect other animals? Which words imitate the sounds other animals make as the lion passes by?

In this poem, what one animal can look at the lion without fear? Is he able to look directly? When *he* looks, what does he see?

✶ ✶ ✶

> Stubborn woodpecker . . .
>   Still hammering
>   At twilight
> At that single spot
>
> —ISSA

What is the woodpecker doing that makes him seem stubborn? How useful is his action?

Do people ever behave like the woodpecker?

✶ ✶ ✶

Have you ever watched a monkey? Could you guess his thoughts from his actions?

> The long night;
> The monkey thinks how
>   To catch hold of the moon.
>
> —SHIKI

What could a monkey be doing, to look as if he wants to catch hold of the moon? Can he catch the moon? Why do you think the poet called it a *long* night?

Do people ever stare at the moon? When? Do people ever have dreams as impossible as the monkey's thoughts?

Why do you think there are both lambs and tigers in the world? Would it be better if there were lambs, but no tigers?

THE TYGER

Tyger! Tyger! burning bright
In the forests of the night,
What immortal hand or eye
Could frame thy fearful symmetry?

In what distant deeps or skies
Burnt the fire of thine eyes?
On what wings dare he aspire?
What the hand dare seize the fire?

And what shoulder, and what art,
Could twist the sinews of thy heart?
And when thy heart began to beat,
What dread hand? and what dread feet?

What the hammer? what the chain?
In what furnace was thy brain?
What the anvil? what dread grasp
Dare its deadly terrors clasp?

When the stars threw down their spears,
And water'd heaven with their tears,
Did he smile his work to see?
Did he who made the Lamb make thee?

Tyger! Tyger! burning bright
In the forests of the night,
What immortal hand or eye
Dare frame thy fearful symmetry?

—WILLIAM BLAKE

How many ways can you think of in which a tiger might be said to be "burning bright"? For example, what color is he? How does he live?

Where does the Tyger live? Why does he belong in that place?

In the third stanza, "dread hand" probably refers to the hand of the Tyger's creator, but "dread feet" to the Tyger himself. Why would Blake call the hand of the creator, or the grasp of the creator in stanza four, "dread" like the Tyger himself? What characteristics do the Tyger and his creator seem to have in common?

What tools did the creator use? What things are usually made with such tools? Why might the creator need such tools to make the Tyger?

How did the rest of nature react when the Tyger was created? What do these reactions show about the Tyger?

Why would Blake repeat the first stanza as the last stanza? Why do you think he changed one word in the last stanza?

Why do you think Blake wrote questions rather than statements about the creation of the Tyger?

People

In life you get to know people in three main ways: (1) by what they say; (2) by what they do; and (3) by what others say about them. Then, as long as you are acquainted with them, you never finish discovering new things about them.

No poem portraying a person, then, can show you everything about him. The poet usually tries to give a strong impression of the person. He may describe only one characteristic, if it is important. Or he may give many little hints. Whichever he does, his description will never be complete. For instance, how much can you know about the personality of a six-month baby?

SLIPPERY

The six month child
Fresh from the tub
Wriggles in our hands.
This is our fish child.
Give her a nickname: Slippery.

—CARL SANDBURG

In what ways is this child like a fish? Does she seem very different from other babies her age?

Have you ever watched a tiny baby in its mother's arms? How did it move its hands? Did the movement remind you of anything?

MARY BLY

I sit here, doing nothing, alone, worn out by long winter.
I feel the light breath of the newborn child.
Her face is smooth as the side of an apricot,
Eyes quick as her blond mother's hands.
She has full, soft, red hair, and as she lies quiet
In her tall mother's arms, her delicate hands
Weave back and forth.
I feel the seasons changing beneath me,
Under the floor.
She is braiding the waters of air into the plaited manes
Of happy colts.
They canter, without making a sound, along the shores
Of melting snow.

—JAMES WRIGHT

What makes the side of an apricot smooth? Is a baby's face smooth in the same way? How else might a baby's face be like an apricot?

How do a baby's hands weave? What did the poet imagine her to be doing? Why does he call what she is braiding "waters of air"?

When colts canter, how do they move? Why do you think the colts in the poem don't make a sound? What is happening to the snow in the last line?

How would you feel, if you were imagining the colts pictured in this poem? How does the poet *say* he feels in the first line? How does he seem to feel in the last six lines? Why have his feelings changed?

Have you ever discovered that an ordinary-looking person possessed surprising talents?

OLD FLORIST

That hump of a man bunching chrysanthemums
Or pinching-back asters, or planting azaleas,
Tamping and stamping dirt into pots,—
How he could flick and pick
Rotten leaves or yellowy petals,
Or scoop out a weed close to flourishing roots,
Or make the dust buzz with a light spray,
Or drown a bug in one spit of tobacco juice,
Or fan life into wilted sweet-peas with his hat,
Or stand all night watering roses, his feet blue in rubber
   boots.

—THEODORE ROETHKE

What would a "hump of a man" look like? What could the old florist do? Which activity would be most interesting to watch?

What rhyming words do you find *inside* lines? How do the rhyming sounds fit the motions of the florist? Which words imitate the sounds they mean?

Why might the old florist "stand all night watering roses"? Would he be comfortable?

Would the old florist be an interesting person to know?

What kinds of people make good neighbors in school? At home? In the world?

PORTRAIT BY A NEIGHBOUR

Before she has her floor swept
    Or her dishes done,
Any day you'll find her
    A-sunning in the sun!

It's long after midnight
    Her key's in the lock,
And you never see her chimney smoke
    Till past ten o'clock!

She digs in her garden
    With a shovel and a spoon,
She weeds her lazy lettuce
    By the light of the moon,

She walks up the walk
    Like a woman in a dream,
She forgets she borrowed butter
    And pays you back cream!

Her lawn looks like a meadow,
    And if she mows the place
She leaves the clover standing
    And the Queen Anne's lace!

—EDNA ST. VINCENT MILLAY

Would you mind having a neighbor like this one?

What adjectives could you use to describe the neighbor? What action of hers caused you to think of each adjective?

Do you think Edna St. Vincent Millay likes her neighbor?

What kind of housewife would be the exact opposite of Edna St. Vincent Millay's neighbor?

THE HOUSEWIFE'S LAMENT

One day I was walking, I heard a complaining,
And saw an old woman the picture of gloom.
She gazed at the mud on her doorstep ('twas raining)
And this was her song as she wielded her broom.
> CHORUS:
> Oh, life is a toil and love is a trouble,
> Beauty will fade and riches will flee,
> Pleasures they dwindle and prices they double,
> And nothing is as I would wish it to be.

There's too much of worriment goes to a bonnet,
There's too much of ironing goes to a shirt,
There's nothing that pays for the time you waste on it,
There's nothing that lasts us but trouble and dirt.
> (CHORUS)

There are worms on the cherries and slugs on the roses,
And ants in the sugar and mice in the pies,
The rubbish of spiders no mortal supposes
And ravaging roaches and damaging flies.
> (CHORUS)

With grease and with grime from corner to center,
Forever at war and forever alert,
No rest for a day lest the enemy enter,
I spend my whole life in a struggle with dirt.
> (CHORUS)

74

Last night in my dreams I was stationed forever
On a far little rock in the midst of the sea,
My one chance of life was a ceaseless endeavour
To sweep off the waves as they swept over me.
   (CHORUS)

Alas! 'Twas no dream; ahead I behold it,
I see I am helpless my fate to avert.—
She lay down her broom, her apron she folded,
She lay down and died and was buried in dirt.
   (CHORUS)

                      —AMERICAN FOLK SONG

Why is the old woman so gloomy? Would her troubles bother you? Do you agree with her views about life, as she keeps expressing them in the chorus?

How is her nightmare related to her life? Why does the song make such a point of saying she was buried in dirt?

From the housewife's song, can you tell what a *lament* is?

SCRUBWOMAN

One shoulder lower,
with unsure step like a bear erect,
the smell of the wet black rags that she cleans with
    about her.

Scratching with four stiff fingers her half-bald head,
    smiling.

—CHARLES REZNIKOFF

How does the poet say the scrubwoman moves? Is the rhythm of the poem regular or irregular? The length of the lines? How do both fit their subject?

Would the smell of her cleaning cloths be unpleasant or pleasant?

Why do you think she is smiling? Do you think the poet likes the scrubwoman?

A psalm is a song of praise. What people would you choose to praise?

PSALM OF THOSE WHO GO FORTH BEFORE DAYLIGHT

The policeman buys shoes slow and careful; the teamster
buys gloves slow and careful; they take care of their
feet and hands; they live on their feet and hands.

The milkman never argues; he works alone and no one
speaks to him; the city is asleep when he is on the job;
he puts a bottle on six hundred porches and calls it a
day's work; he climbs two hundred wooden stairways;
two horses are company for him; he never argues.

The rolling-mill men and the sheet-steel men are brothers
of cinders; they empty cinders out of their shoes after
the day's work; they ask their wives to fix burnt holes
in the knees of their trousers; their necks and ears are
covered with a smut; they scour their necks and ears;
they are brothers of cinders.

—CARL SANDBURG

What people does this psalm praise? Could the poet have in-
cluded the scrubwoman in his psalm?

What combinations of words are repeated in the first stanza?
Why are these words important enough to be repeated?

What adjectives best describe the milkman's job? Why does
Sandburg call the steel workers *brothers* of cinders?

Do these jobs sound pleasant? Why do you think Carl Sandburg wanted to praise the people who do them?

In Ireland in 1845, the potato crop failed, and famine followed. Many men and women were forced to leave their homes and roam the roads.

AN OLD WOMAN OF THE ROADS

Oh, to have a little house!
To own the hearth and stool and all!
The heaped up sods upon the fire,
The pile of turf against the wall!

To have a clock with weights and chains
And pendulum swinging up and down!
A dresser filled with shining delph,
Speckled and white and blue and brown!

I could be busy all the day
Clearing and sweeping hearth and floor,
And fixing on their shelf again
My white and blue and speckled store!

I could be quiet there at night
Beside the fire and by myself,
Sure of a bed and loth to leave
The ticking clock and the shining delph!

Och! but I'm weary of mist and dark,
And roads where there's never a house nor bush,
And tired I am of the bog and road,
And the crying wind and the lonesome hush!

And I am praying to God on high,
And I am praying Him night and day,
For a little house—a house of my own—
Out of the wind's and the rain's way.

—PADRAIC COLUM

Why does this old woman want a little house more than anything else?

Can you tell what *delph* (sometimes spelled *delft*) is, from the way the woman describes it? Why does she mention it so many times?

What other things does she mention more than once? Why?

✓ ✓ ✓

HEAR MY VOICE

Hear my voice, Birds of War!
I prepare a feast for you to feed on;
I see you cross the enemy's lines;
Like you I shall go.
I wish the swiftness of your wings;
I wish the vengeance of your claws;
I muster my friends;
I follow your flight.
Ho, you young men warriors,
Bear your angers to the place of fighting!

—AMERICAN INDIAN SONG

How does dancing make you feel? Would most musicians enjoy playing dance music?

THE FIDDLER OF DOONEY

When I play on my fiddle in Dooney,
Folk dance like a wave of the sea;
My cousin is priest in Kilvarnet,
My brother in Mocharabuiee.*

I passed my brother and cousin:
They read in their books of prayer;
I read in my book of songs
I bought at the Sligo fair.

When we come at the end of time
To Peter sitting in state,
He will smile on the three old spirits,
But call me first through the gate;

For the good are always the merry,
Save by an evil chance,
And the merry love the fiddle,
And the merry love to dance:

And when the folk there spy me,
They will all come up to me,
With 'Here is the fiddler of Dooney!'
And dance like a wave of the sea.

—WILLIAM BUTLER YEATS

(* Pronounced as if spelt "Mockrabwee.")

The places mentioned in this poem are all in Ireland. Since Ireland is an island, the people are familiar with the sea. How do waves of the sea move? What does the comparison show about how the people of Dooney dance?

The fiddler imagines himself and his brother and cousin meeting St. Peter on the Day of Judgment, when all souls are to be sent either to Heaven or to Hell. How does he expect to be treated differently? Do you agree that he should be treated differently?

↗ ↗ ↗

Do ordinary people know what famous people are really like?

ABRAHAM LINCOLN
1809-1865

Lincoln was a long man.
He liked out of doors.
He liked the wind blowing
And the talk in country stores.

He liked telling stories,
He liked telling jokes.
"Abe's quite a character,"
Said quite a lot of folks.

Lots of folks in Springfield
Saw him every day,
Walking down the street
In his gaunt, long way.

Shawl around his shoulders,
Letters in his hat.
"That's Abe Lincoln."
They thought no more than that.

Knew that he was honest,
Guessed that he was odd,
Knew he had a cross wife
Though she was a Todd.

Knew he had three little boys
Who liked to shout and play,
Knew he had a lot of debts
It took him years to pay.

Knew his clothes and knew his house.
"That's his office, here.
Blame good lawyer, on the whole,
Though he's sort of queer.

"Sure, he went to Congress, once.
But he didn't stay.
Can't expect us all to be
Smart as Henry Clay.

"Need a man for troubled times?
Well, I guess we do.
Wonder who we'll ever find?
Yes—I wonder who."

That is how they met and talked,
Knowing and unknowing.
Lincoln was the green pine.
Lincoln kept on growing.

—STEVEN VINCENT BENÉT
and ROSEMARY BENÉT

Who is saying the words in quotation marks? What does this voice know about Lincoln? What things do you know about Lincoln that the voice doesn't mention? Why do you think it leaves those things out? Does the voice admire Lincoln whole-heartedly?

In what particular way does the poem *say* Lincoln was like the green pine? How else does the poem *show* him to be like the green pine? For instance, is a pine a squat tree or a tall one, even when it's young? What do we mean when we call a baseball pitcher "green"? How much political experience had Lincoln had?

Actually, this poem· doesn't say Lincoln was *like* the green pine; it says he *was* the green pine. But Lincoln, a man, can't be *exactly* the same as a green pine, a tree. If you think of Lincoln and the green pine each as a circle and try to put the two circles together, they don't fit exactly. Rather, they look something like this:

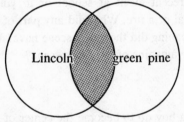

The shaded area where the two circles overlap represents the ways in which Lincoln and the green pine are like each other. But there are large parts of both circles that don't overlap at all. These parts represent the ways in which the man and the green pine are entirely different.

Though the circles of some comparisons may overlap more than these two, no comparison of any two things or people can fit exactly. Why not?

✓ ✓ ✓

Scenes

Things always happen somewhere; nothing happens nowhere. Even an astronaut walks in space, and space is a place with particular qualities. The author of a play sets the scene for the events of his play. Occasionally, a playwright may decide not to have any scenery at all, but then the lack of scenery is just as remarkable as the apparent emptiness of outer space.

A poem, too, may set the scene for a drama. The events of the drama happen in a particular place at a particular time. To describe the scene and event, the poet will often compare *directly*. A direct comparison says that one thing *is* another or is *like* another.

Sometimes, though, the comparison is *indirect*. The poet will give you clues, but you'll have to decide for yourself exactly what is being compared to what. Through both direct and indirect comparisons, the poet can show you what the scene means to him.

Think of a recent event at school or in your neighborhood, perhaps a carnival or a fire. What did any part of the scene remind you of? What meaning did the entire scene have? What comparison might express the meaning of the entire scene?

What might a boy do to become the center of everyone's attention?

CHILD ON TOP OF A GREENHOUSE

The wind billowing out the seat of my britches,
My feet crackling splinters of glass and dried putty,
The half-grown chrysanthemums staring up like accusers,
Up through the streaked glass, flashing with sunlight,
A few white clouds all rushing eastward,
A line of elms plunging and tossing like horses,
And everyone, everyone pointing up and shouting!

—THEODORE ROETHKE

Do you think the boy enjoyed or feared the situation? What in the poem makes you think so?

What particular details make this scene stand out from any other? What parts of the scene does the boy compare to other things? What do these comparisons show you about his feelings?

Change all of the *-ing* word endings (except *flashing*) to *-ed* endings and read the poem that way. Why do you suppose Roethke used *-ing* words rather than *-ed* ones?

↗ ↗ ↗

What is the saddest sound you've ever heard? Where did you hear it? What did it sound like?

LOST

Desolate and lone
All night long on the lake
Where fog trails and mist creeps,
The whistle of a boat
Calls and cries unendingly,
Like some lost child
In tears and trouble
Hunting the harbor's breast
And the harbor's eyes.

—CARL SANDBURG

How does reading this description make you feel?

How might a boat whistle sound like a crying child? How would you feel if you heard a child crying unendingly?

Who would a lost child cry for? What is the harbor being compared to?

What is the smallest sound you've ever heard? What did it sound like?

SPLINTER

The voice of the last cricket
across the first frost
is one kind of good-by.
It is so thin a splinter of singing.

—CARL SANDBURG

To understand what kind of good-by the cricket's song is, think of other sounds that might mean good-by—for example, the whistle of a jet take-off. How would those sounds be like or be different from the cricket's voice?

What word tells you how the cricket's song is like a splinter? Would the song be like a splinter in any other way?

✓ ✓ ✓

Have you ever watched people speaking to each other, when you couldn't hear their words?

THE WHITE HORSE

The youth walks up to the white horse, to put its halter on, and the horse looks at him in silence.
They are so silent they are in another world.

—D. H. LAWRENCE

What sounds would a boy usually make as he puts a halter on a horse? What sounds would the horse make?

Do you think the observer is nearby or far away? How does watching make him feel? What hints at his feeling?

Haiku

For many hundreds of years, Japanese poets have been picturing scenes from nature. To picture these scenes, they originated a special form of poetry called *haiku.*

> He washes his horse
> With the setting sun
> In the autumn sea.

> —SHIKI

Why does it look as if the man is actually washing the horse with the setting sun?

✶ ✶ ✶

> Camellia-petal
>   Fell in silent dawn . . .
>   Spilling
> A water-jewel

> —BASHO

What is the "water-jewel" spilled by the camellia petal? When did the petal fall? What mood is suggested in the haiku?

✶ ✶ ✶

> A world of dew:
> Yet within the dewdrops—
> Quarrels.

> —ISSA

What world could the poet mean by "A world of dew"? Why does the second line start with *yet*?

What kinds of quarrels might be within dewdrops?

Haiku not only help you see. They sometimes help you hear. What special sounds are the subjects of these next haiku?

Girls planting paddy:
Only their song
Free of the mud.

—RAIZAN

All its advertisements
Given over to the wind—
The windbell shop.

—ANONYMOUS

Two ducks swim to the shore
The quacking duck and the blowing wind
Wrinkle the face of the water.

—HIROSHIGE

Which haiku imitates a sound? How do the others show the qualities of the sounds they describe?

Haiku are like bells rung; the main subject is surrounded with echoes. As an experiment, to catch some of the echoes, choose a haiku you like particularly. Try to write out an ordinary statement of every meaning you think the haiku hints at.

Can you find just the right words to say what the poem means? Count the words in your statement, compared to the number in the haiku itself.

✓ ✓ ✓

Haiku appeal to all five senses, not only to sight and hearing.

How cool cut hay smells
when carried through the farm gate
as the sun comes up!

—BONCHO

Under cherry-trees
Soup, the salad,
Fish and all . . .
Seasoned with petals

—BASHO

See the morning breeze
Ruffling his so
Silky hair . . .
Cool caterpillar

—BUSON

Which senses do these haiku appeal to?

The Shape of Haiku

There are special rules for the shape of a Japanese haiku. Harry Behn followed these rules in a haiku about haiku, which he wrote in English.

The first line has five syllables:

1 2 3 4 5
A spark in the sun,

The second line has seven syllables:

1   23 4 5 6 7
this tiny flower has roots

The third line again has five syllables:

1   2 3 4 5
deep in the cool earth.

Some of the haiku translations in this book follow the Japanese rules, and some don't.

Which senses do the next three haiku appeal to?

After the shower . . .
    Spring-enchanted
    Sparrow-folk
Chatter on the eaves

                —UKO

Frog-school competing
with lark-school at dusk softly
    in the art of song . . .

                —SHIKI

Insects one hears—
    and one hears the talk of men—
    with different ears.

                —WAFU

How is hearing the talk of men different from hearing insects?
Do human beings ever act like the sparrows or the frogs and larks?
What comparisons are hidden in these haiku?

A Note on Translation

Have you been wondering how you could read Japanese poems in English? The Japanese language, in which all these haiku were originally written, is very different from English in its sounds and in the order of its words.

The original poem sets the subject and tells what the poet noticed about the subject. If the original haiku made a statement or asked a question, then the translation should make a statement or ask a question. The translator's job is to choose English words that sound right to him for the subject and the idea of the poem. In the haiku you've read, have you noticed any words or lines that sound especially right to you? If you have, you're appreciating the translation, not the original poem.

The next two haiku are different translations of the same original poem:

An old silent pond . . .
A frog jumps into the pond,
   splash! Silence again

—BASHO

Old dark sleepy pool . . .
   Quick unexpected
   Frog
Goes plop! Watersplash!

—BASHO

Is what happens in both translations basically the same? What different words are used for the same idea? Is either translation a single ordinary sentence? Which translation do you prefer? Do you have any special reason for preferring it, or do you just like it without being able to give any reason? Why can't you say which translation is the only right one?

✓ ✓ ✓

Most of the translated haiku you've read were about nature. The Japanese who wrote them expressed their wonder about the everyday nature that surrounded them. Contemporary poets sometimes write haiku-like poems about the wonders that surround us today.

This smoky winter morning—
do not despise the green jewel shining among the twigs
because it is a traffic light.

—CHARLES REZNIKOFF

✓ ✓ ✓

At the shouts and cheers
The grandstand seems
Just about to collapse.

—ANONYMOUS
(Japanese)

If there's a bit of grit in the spinach, or if sand gets into the potato salad on a picnic, adults sometimes tell children that each of us will eat a peck of dirt in his lifetime. The saying was a bit different for Robert Frost, who lived in San Francisco as a boy.

A PECK OF GOLD

Dust always blowing about the town,
Except when sea-fog laid it down,
And I was one of the children told
Some of the blowing dust was gold.

All the dust the wind blew high
Appeared like gold in the sunset sky,
But I was one of the children told
Some of the dust was really gold.

Such was life in the Golden Gate:
Gold dusted all we drank and ate,
And I was one of the children told,
"We all must eat our peck of gold."

—ROBERT FROST

What about its geography or history would make it appropriate for San Francisco children to be told, "We all must eat our peck of gold"?

How many times does the word *gold* or *golden* appear in each stanza? As the poem continues, does the poet seem to accept the idea that some of the dust was really gold?

What would it be like to spend your childhood in a golden town?

Ecco is an Italian word, which may be translated to mean *look, see, behold.*

e
cco the uglies
t

s
ub
sub

urba
n skyline on earth between whose d
owdy

hou
se
s

l
ooms an eggyellow smear of wintry sunse
t

—E. E. CUMMINGS

Have you ever been caught in a thunder-and-lightning rain storm? How did it begin?

THE WIND BEGUN TO ROCK THE GRASS

The Wind begun to rock the Grass
With threatening Tunes and low—
He threw a Menace at the Earth—
A Menace at the Sky.

The Leaves unhooked themselves from Trees—
And started all abroad
The Dust did scoop itself like Hands
And threw away the Road.

The Wagons quickened on the Streets
The Thunder hurried slow—
The Lightning showed a Yellow Beak
And then a livid Claw.

The Birds put up the Bars to Nests—
The Cattle fled to Barns—
There came one drop of Giant Rain
And then as if the Hands

That held the Dams had parted hold
The Waters Wrecked the Sky,
But overlooked my Father's House—
Just quartering a Tree—

—EMILY DICKINSON

How did this storm begin? How much damage did it cause?
What pronoun would you usually use in talking about the wind? What pronoun does Emily Dickinson use? She talks about the wind as if it were a—what?

What else does she talk about in the same way? How does her use of capital letters fit the way she talks?

What comparisons picture the dust and the lightning? What does the storm as a whole seem to be like?

THE WIND BLOWS THE RAIN

The wind blows the rain into our faces
as we go down the hillside
upon rusted cans and old newspapers,
past the tree on whose bare branches
the boys have hung iron hoops,
until we reach at last the crushed earthworms
stretched and stretching on the wet sidewalk.
—CHARLES REZNIKOFF

Which of these words would fit this description of the scene: exhilarating, depressing, interesting, alive, beautiful, accurate? Can you think of other words to fit the description?

Where could you see a scene like this? What details give you clues? Which senses do these details appeal to?

When you read this poem aloud, does the rhythm of the words sound like normal, natural speech or like the words to a song? What poems with each kind of rhythm do you remember especially?

How does a scene look different when it's reflected in water?

WATER PICTURE

In the pond in the park
all things are doubled:
Long buildings hang and
wriggle gently. Chimneys
are bent legs bouncing
on clouds below. A flag
wags like a fishhook
down there in the sky.

The arched stone bridge
is an eye, with underlid
in the water. In its lens
dip crinkled heads with hats
that don't fall off. Dogs go by,
barking on their backs.
A baby, taken to feed the
ducks, dangles upside-down,
a pink balloon for a buoy.

Treetops deploy a haze of
cherry bloom for roots,
where birds coast belly-up
in the glass bowl of a hill;
from its bottom a bunch
of peanut-munching children
are suspended by their
sneakers, waveringly.

A swan, with twin necks
forming the figure three,
steers between two dimpled
towers doubled. Fondly
hissing, she kisses herself,
and all the scene is troubled:
water-windows splinter,
tree-limbs tangle, the bridge
folds like a fan.

—MAY SWENSON

4

POEMS
EXPRESS
FEELINGS

Hᴀᴠᴇ you ever tried to tell someone else how you feel? How excited, happy, sad, lonely, dull, dizzy, or delirious you feel? (What other feelings could you list?) Why was it hard to express your feeling? How did you express it?

Everyone feels many small emotions every day. Discovering that there are strawberries for breakfast can make you happy, even before you taste them. Or, if your best friend isn't waiting as usual to walk to school with you, you feel unhappy. At school you learn that your friend is sick, and you forget your own moment of unhappiness because you're hoping your friend will get well.

Sometimes your emotion is big, not small. Then it affects the way you feel about everything for quite a long time. You may feel special because someone likes you and shows his liking. Or someone may go away, leaving an emptiness behind.

It's easier to tell someone about the small emotion than about the big one. Happiness, you can say, is fresh strawberries for breakfast. Loneliness is walking to school by yourself. How else might you finish the sentences: "Happiness is . . ." or "Loneliness is . . ."?

When a poet expresses a small emotion or mood, he tries to find something that will picture it for you. The right picture will help you understand his feeling. If he can find just the right words for his picture, you can even share his feeling.

It's harder to tell about liking someone or missing someone, because those feelings are complicated. They are several things all at once and for a long time.

When a poet writes a poem expressing a big emotion, he tries to find actions or situations big enough to show the emotion. For instance, suppose a poet wants to tell how he feels about the death of his son. He remembers his son's life— what the boy said and did. The poet doesn't tell everything about his son. Instead, he might describe one thing he misses especially. The one thing comes to stand for everything his son did and was, just as an "A" on your report card stands for everything you did to earn it.

What happens to you inside when you can tell someone how you feel? What happens to you when someone succeeds in telling you how *he* feels? Why would a poet want to write a poem picturing a feeling?

Bright and Dark Moods

Pippa is a young Italian girl who starts her holiday with a song.

PIPPA'S SONG

The year's at the spring
And day's at the morn;
Morning's at seven;
The hill-side's dew-pearled;
The lark's on the wing;
The snail's on the thorn:
God's in his heaven—
All's right with the world!

—ROBERT BROWNING

How does Pippa say she feels about her holiday? How do the things she mentions show her feeling? For example, does the snail belong on the thorn? What has thorns? Where is the snail?

How would it feel to be a mouse in a jungle? When would it be safe to come out of hiding?

MADAME MOUSE TROTS

Madame Mouse trots,
Grey in the black night!
Madame Mouse trots:
Furred is the light.
The elephant-trunks
Trumpet from the sea . . .
Grey in the black night
The mouse trots free.
Hoarse as a dog's bark
The heavy leaves are furled . . .
The cat's in his cradle,
All's well with the world!

—EDITH SITWELL

How is Madame Mouse's feeling like Pippa's?

How many times does Edith Sitwell say that Madame Mouse trots? What other verbs can you think of to tell how a mouse moves? Why do you think the poet chose to say that Madame Mouse *trots?*

What other animals are mentioned? Is there any relationship between what those animals are doing and the way Madame Mouse feels?

What would "furred" light look like? What words describe the leaves? What are they compared to? Do you think such leaves would be slick or velvety or rough in texture? How do both the light and the leaves fit with what the other animals are doing?

What other line is repeated? How are the colors of Madame Mouse's world different from the colors suggested in Pippa's song?

l(a

le
af
fa

ll

s)
one
l

iness

—E. E. CUMMINGS

✓ ✓ ✓

At this dreary inn
A hound keeps
Wailing . . . like me
Lonely in the rain?

—BASHO

✓ ✓ ✓

Crossing it alone
  In cold moonlight . . .
    The brittle bridge
Echoes my footsteps

                          —TAIGI

What mood do all three of these poems express? What picture
does each one use to show the mood? Which poem makes you feel
the mood most strongly?

"Border Songs" are the songs of ancient Oriental warriors.

BORDER SONGS

1

His golden arrow is tipped with hawk's feathers,
His embroidered silk flag has a tail like a swallow.
One man, arising, gives a new order
To the answering shout of a thousand tents.

2

Let feasting begin in the wild camp!
Let bugles cry our victory!
Let us drink, let us dance in our golden armour!
Let us thunder on rivers and hills with our drums!

—LI LUN

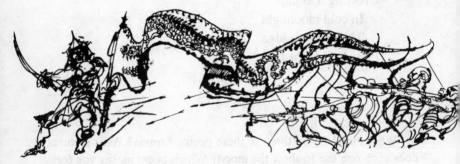

What mood are the warriors expressing?

How do the descriptions of the arrow, the flag, and the armour contribute to the expression of that mood? What actions contribute to the mood?

When do you think the battle occurred: before the poem starts, between the stanzas, or after the poem ends?

106

Scampering over saucers—
The sound of a rat.
Cold, cold.

—BUSON

What would be "cold" about a rat running over saucers? Why do you suppose the translator said *scampering* rather than *running?*

✔ ✔ ✔

One man and one fly
buzzing alone together
in a sunny room . . .

—ISSA

Which words establish the mood of this haiku?

✔ ✔ ✔

How might you feel, going home alone on a moonlit night?

From watching the moon
I turned
And my friendly old
Shadow led me home.

—SHIKI

What word sums up the feeling expressed in this haiku?

Have you ever had an experience that turned an upside-down day right-side up? Was what happened a big thing or a little thing?

DUST OF SNOW

The way a crow
Shook down on me
The dust of snow
From a hemlock tree

Has given my heart
A change of mood
And saved some part
Of a day I had rued.

—ROBERT FROST

Was it a large or small happening that changed the poet's mood? Why do you think the happening affected him?

If you were illustrating this poem, which medium would you use: pen and ink, water colors, tempera paints, charcoal, or oils? How do the colors in the poem fit its meaning?

What kinds of things make you unhappy? If you're unhappy, what do you do to help yourself feel better?

DEPRESSED BY A BOOK OF BAD POETRY, I WALK TOWARD AN UNUSED PASTURE AND INVITE THE INSECTS TO JOIN ME

Relieved, I let the book fall behind a stone.
I climb a slight rise of grass.
I do not want to disturb the ants
Who are walking single file up the fence post,
Carrying small white petals,
Casting shadows so frail that I can see through them.
I close my eyes for a moment, and listen.
The old grasshoppers
Are tired, they leap heavily now,
Their thighs are burdened.
I want to hear them, they have clear sounds to make.
Then lovely, far off, a dark cricket begins
In the maple trees.

—JAMES WRIGHT

What does the poet do to get away from the book? Why do you think he doesn't want to disturb the ants? What sights and sounds please him?

Which parts of this poem are almost like haiku? Could you add anything to the parts to make complete haiku? Would you want to change any words or leave any out?

Imagine a poem this poet would find depressing. Judging from the things he likes in this poem, what would you guess the depressing poem might be about? How might it sound?

POEMS OF SOLITARY DELIGHTS

What a delight it is
When on the bamboo matting
In my grass-thatched hut,
All on my own,
I make myself at ease.

What a delight it is
When, skimming through the pages
Of a book, I discover
A man written of there
Who is just like me.

What a delight it is
When everyone admits
It's a very difficult book,
And I understand it
With no trouble at all.

What a delight it is
When a guest you cannot stand
Arrives, then says to you
"I'm afraid I can't stay long,"
And soon goes home.

—TACHIBANA AKEMI

may i be gay

like every lark
who lifts his life

from all the dark

who wings his why

beyond because
and sings an if

of day to yes

—E. E. CUMMINGS

What mood does this poem express? What basic comparison
pictures the mood?

Can you ask any "why" questions which no one, not even you,
could answer completely? For example, the lark, if he could think
and speak, might ask, "Why do I fly?" or "Why do I sing?" How
do "why" questions like these, or like yours, go "beyond because"?

Suppose you ask permission to do something. Which answer
would you rather hear: one that says, "Yes"; or one that starts,
"If . . ."? How might "An if of day" be different from "yes"?
For instance, would a day that starts with an "if" be likely to be
sunny or rainy, happy or unhappy? Can you know for sure? What
happens to the day when the lark sings?

What kinds of sound repetition help hold the words of this
poem together memorably?

Love and Loss

A pavane is a dance with a slow, stately rhythm. Like the minuet, it came from France.

(Don't let the phrase "for the Nursery" in the title mislead you. Things important at the beginning of life are important all through it.)

A PAVANE FOR THE NURSERY

Now touch the air softly,
Step gently. One, two . . .
I'll love you till roses
Are robin's-egg blue;
I'll love you till gravel
Is eaten for bread,
And lemons are orange,
And lavender's red.

Now touch the air softly,
Swing gently the broom.
I'll love you till windows
Are all of a room;
And the table is laid,
And the table is bare,
And the ceiling reposes
On bottomless air.

I'll love you till Heaven
Rips the stars from his coat,
And the Moon rows away in
A glass-bottomed boat;
And Orion steps down
Like a diver below,
And Earth is ablaze,
And Ocean aglow.

So touch the air softly,
And swing the broom high.
We will dust the gray mountains,
And sweep the blue sky;
And I'll love you as long
As the furrow the plow,
As However is Ever,
And Ever is Now.

—WILLIAM JAY SMITH

Who do you think is speaking in this poem? Who might he or
she be speaking to? What does the rhythm of the pavane suggest
they might be doing?

When you first read this poem, what kind of sense does it
seem to make? The speaker imagines happenings that might mark
the end of love. Which of these happenings seems most unlikely?
When will the speaker's love end?

What line is repeated? Why might a person in love be likely
to act as the line directs him to act?

How are you to step and swing the broom in the first two
stanzas? In the last stanza? What kinds of things do the last two
stanzas picture, as compared to the things in the first two stanzas?
How is the feeling expressed in the last two stanzas different from
the feeling expressed in the first two?

In the King Arthur stories, Elaine, the young girl who lived in Astolat Castle, died for love of the knight, Launcelot, who did not return her love.

LAUNCELOT WITH BICYCLE

Her window looks upon the lane.
From it, anonymous and shy,
Twice daily she can see him plain,
Wheeling heroic by.
She droops her cheek against the pane
And gives a little sigh.

Above him maples at their bloom
Shake April pollen down like stars
While he goes whistling past her room
Toward unimagined wars,
A tennis visor for his plume,
Scornful of handlebars.

And, counting over in her mind
His favors, gleaned like windfall fruit
(A morning when he spoke her kind,
An afterschool salute,
A number that she helped him find,
Once, for his paper route),

Sadly she twists a stubby braid
And closer to the casement leans—
A wistful and a lily maid
In moccasins and jeans,
Despairing from the seventh grade
To match his lordly teens.

And so she grieves in Astolat
(Where other girls have grieved the same)
For being young and therefore not
Sufficient to his fame—
Who will by summer have forgot
Grief, April, and his name.

—PHYLLIS McGINLEY

What words in the poem show the mood of the girl? What is
the boy's mood, as his actions show it? How does the description
of the season fit with both moods?

What contacts has the girl had with the boy? What has she
done with the memory of those meetings?

What words in the poem suggest the time of King Arthur, when
knights were brave and ladies were fair? How is the situation in
this poem like the story of Elaine and Launcelot? How is it different?

If you love someone, what might he or she seem to be like to you?

TO A GOLDEN-HAIRED GIRL IN A LOUISIANA TOWN

You are a sunrise,
If a star should rise instead of the sun.
You are a moonrise,
If a star should come, in the place of the moon.
You are the Spring,
If a face should bloom,
Instead of an apple-bough.
You are my love
If your heart is as kind
As your young eyes now.

—VACHEL LINDSAY

What things does the poet say the girl is to him? What special qualities do all those things have in common?

What "if" statements does he add to his statements about the girl? Why do you think he adds them?

TO AN ISLE IN THE WATER

Shy one, shy one,
Shy one of my heart,
She moves in the firelight
Pensively apart.

She carries in the dishes,
And lays them in a row.
To an isle in the water
With her would I go.

She carries in the candles,
And lights the curtained room,
Shy in the doorway
And shy in the gloom;

And shy as a rabbit,
Helpful and shy.
To an isle in the water
With her would I fly.

—WILLIAM BUTLER YEATS

SHE DWELT AMONG THE UNTRODDEN WAYS

She dwelt among the untrodden ways
   Beside the springs of Dove,
A maid whom there were none to praise
   And very few to love:

A violet by a mossy stone
   Half hidden from the eye!
—Fair as a star, when only one
   Is shining in the sky.

She lived unknown, and few could know
   When Lucy ceased to be;
But she is in her grave, and, oh,
   The difference to me!

           —WILLIAM WORDSWORTH

How is Lucy like the girl in "To an Isle in the Water"? How is she like the golden-haired Louisiana girl? How is she different from either of them?

What do the comparisons in the poem show about Lucy's character? What do they show about the poet's feelings?

118

An elegy is a song of mourning for someone who has died.

LITTLE ELEGY
for a child who skipped rope

Here lies resting, out of breath,
Out of turns, Elizabeth
Whose quicksilver toes not quite
Cleared the whirring edge of night.

Earth whose circles round us skim
Till they catch the lightest limb,
Shelter now Elizabeth
And for her sake trip up death.

—X. J. KENNEDY

Which words in the first stanza sound active? What kind of child was Elizabeth? Instead of dying, what seems to have happened to her? What words remain you that this is an elegy?

In the second stanza, how does the poet seem to feel about her death? What does he hope may happen to Elizabeth? Why do you think he makes *death* the last word in the poem?

How does everything in the poem fit the subtitle, *for a child who skipped rope?*

ON HER DEAD SON

In what windy land
    Wanders now
    My little dear
Dragonfly hunter?

—CHIYO-NI

✓ ✓ ✓

TANKA

Since he is too young
To know the way, I would plead:
"Pray, accept this gift,
O Underworld messenger,
And bear the child pick-a-back."

—OKURA
(Translated by Babette Deutsch)

    Are these parents thinking about their children as if the children were alive or dead? How do the parents' thoughts show their feelings?

✓ ✓ ✓

Like dust swirling
At the height of winter,
News of his death.

—KYOSHI

    Who do you think has died? What does the comparison show you about the poet's feelings?

This next song expresses an American Indian husband's sorrow at the death of his wife.

CARRYING MY MIND AROUND

My own mind is very hard to me.
It is just as if I were carrying my mind around.
What is the matter with you?

—AMERICAN INDIAN SONG

DARK GIRL

Easy on your drums,
Easy wind and rain,
And softer on your horns,
She will not dance again.

Come easy little leaves
Without a ghost of sound
From the China trees
To the fallow ground.

Easy, easy drums
And sweet leaves overhead,
Easy wind and rain;
Your dancing girl is dead.

—ARNA BONTEMPS

What does the poet want to have happen? Why do you think
he speaks especially to drums and horns? To wind, rain, and leaves?

LAMENT

Listen, children;
Your father is dead.
From his old coats
I'll make you little jackets;
I'll make you little trousers
From his old pants.
There'll be in his pockets
Things he used to put there.
Keys and pennies
Covered with tobacco;
Dan shall have the pennies
To save in his bank;
Anne shall have the keys
To make a pretty noise with.
Life must go on,
And the dead be forgotten;
Life must go on,
Though good men die;
Anne, eat your breakfast;
Dan take your medicine;
Life must go on;
I forget just why.

—EDNA ST. VINCENT MILLAY

What subjects does the speaker talk about? How do these show
her feelings?

What does the length of the lines show about her feelings? Is
she able to talk easily and smoothly?

What idea does she repeat? Why do you think she repeats it?

TO MY BROTHER MIGUEL: *in memoriam*

Brother, today I sit on the brick bench outside the
   house,
where you make a bottomless emptiness.
I remember we used to play at this hour of the day,
   and mama
would calm us: "There now, boys . . ."

Now I go hide
as before, from all these evening
prayers, and I hope that you will not find me.
In the parlor, the entrance hall, the corridors.
Later, you hide, and I do not find you.
I remember we made each other cry,
brother, in that game.

Miguel, you hid yourself
one night in August, nearly at daybreak,
but instead of laughing when you hid, you were sad.
And your other heart of those dead afternoons
is tired of looking and not finding you. And now
shadows fall on the soul.

Listen, brother, don't be too late
coming out. All right? Mama might worry.

—CESAR VALLEJO
(Translated by John Knoepfle and James Wright)

How does the living boy feel about his brother's death? Which
lines especially reveal his feelings?

Why is he speaking to his brother at this time? Whose heart
might "your other heart of those dead afternoons" be? Why are the
afternoons "dead"?

How do you think the speaker expects Miguel to respond to
the last stanza?

123

5

POEMS
MAKE
FUN

It's Halloween, and spirits stalk the streets. You're on your way to a party, disguised as a bat. Your rubber mask startled even you, the first time you saw an enormous, wrinkled, old mouse staring back at you from the mirror. You were still expecting to see your own face. Then you giggled when you thought of the fun you were going to have surprising the other party-goers.

Now, prepared to terrify everyone at the party, you ring the bell, even though the door is partly open. The house looks dark and deserted. And there's not even a whisper or a sneeze, though you'd expect to hear a gabble of noise coming from a party. Maybe you're too early, or maybe it's the wrong house.

No, it's the right number, and you know you're late, as usual. Besides, why is the door open? You'd better investigate.

You tiptoe in cautiously, just in case you have to make a quick get-away. If it was dark outside, it's even darker inside. You can't see a thing. Suddenly the lights all go on at once, and a whole menagerie of your costumed friends whinny, cackle, grunt, and trumpet, "Surprise!" You're so dazed you forget all about giving your carefully practiced eerie bat cry. Then you join the laughter when you realize the joke's on you. If you haven't been the last person to arrive, you can give your cry to surprise the next arrival.

A poem, too, can make fun by surprising you, most often by making unexpected sounds. For example, it may rhyme unusual words, like *whisk its* and *biscuits*. You chuckle because the words sound funny together. Or perhaps the sound of the rhyme isn't unusual, but the rhyming words make an unexpected kind of sense. They connect two things you would never have thought of putting together, like *home work* and *chrome work*.

Sometimes, too, the rhyming words or other words in a poem aren't ordinary, good English. For instance, a poet may ask a strange-looking animal, "Is those things arms, or is they legs?" Would you ask the question that way? Why might it be all right for the poet to talk like that?

Besides making unexpected sounds or using unusual words, a whole poem can wear a disguise, like your bat costume. At the beginning, the poem may pretend to be one kind of poem, but it ends up as a different kind altogether. It tries to surprise the reader, as your friends surprised you. What makes it fun to be surprised?

Can parents or older people help you with your homework? Why might they have trouble helping you?

ASK DADDY, HE WON'T KNOW

Now that they've abolished chrome work
I'd like to call their attention to home work.
Here it is only three decades since my scholarship was
    famous,
And I'm an ignoramus.
I cannot think which goes sideways and which goes up
    and down, a parallel or a meridian,
Nor do I know the name of him who first translated the
    Bible into Indian, I see him only as an enterprising
    colonial Gideon.
I have difficulty with dates,
To say nothing of the annual rainfall of the Southern
    Central States,
And the only way I can distinguish proper from
    improper fractions
Is by their actions.
Naturally the correct answers are just back of the tip
    of my tongue,

But try to explain that to your young.
I am overwhelmed by their erudite banter,
I am in no condition to differentiate between Tamerlane
and Tam O'Shanter.
I reel, I sway, I am utterly exhausted;
Should you ask me when Chicago was founded I could
only reply I didn't even know it was losted.

—OGDEN NASH

Is there any connection between abolishing chrome work and abolishing home work? Why do you think the poet mentions them together?

Can you set this father straight on any of the facts? How important do you think it is to know all the facts he mentions? Can you tell what "erudite banter" is from the rest of the poem?

Which lines rhyme? Which rhymes seem most unexpected, either in sound or in sense?

Who would you usually expect to give arguments for abolishing home work?

✓ ✓ ✓

What do you think a gnu would look like, judging from the sound of his name?

THE GNU

There's this to Remember about the Gnu:
He closely Resembles—but I can't tell you!

—THEODORE ROETHKE

Who do *you* think the gnu resembles? Why do you think the poet brought up the subject in the first place?

Where might you meet a cockroach?

NURSERY RHYME FOR THE TENDER-HEARTED

Scuttle, scuttle, little roach—
How you run when I approach:
Up above the pantry shelf,
Hastening to secrete yourself.

Most adventurous of vermin,
How I wish I could determine
How you spend your hours of ease,
Perhaps reclining on the cheese.

Cook has gone, and all is dark—
Then the kitchen is your park:
In the garbage heap that she leaves
Do you browse among the tea leaves?

How delightful to suspect
All the places you have trekked:
Does your long antenna whisk its
Gentle tip across the biscuits?

Do you linger, little soul,
Drowsing in our sugar bowl?
Or, abandonment most utter,
Shake a shimmy on the butter?

Do you chant your simple tunes
Swimming in the baby's prunes?
Then, when dawn comes, do you slink
Homeward to the kitchen sink?

Timid roach, why be so shy?
We are brothers, thou and I.
In the midnight, like yourself,
I explore the pantry shelf!

—CHRISTOPHER MORLEY

What word shows how a cockroach moves? What nursery
rhyme does the first stanza imitate? How is the subject of this poem
different from the subject of that nursery rhyme?

Where in the dark kitchen do you think the cockroach spends
most of his time? Why do you think so?

Do you think the poet is making fun of the cockroach? Who
else might he be making fun of? What clue does the title give you?

What kind of television programs come on before suppertime?

DEATH AT SUPPERTIME

Between the dark and the daylight,
  When the night is beginning to lower,
Comes a pause in the day's occupation,
  That is known as the Children's Hour.

Then endeth the skipping and skating,
  The giggles, the tantrums, and tears,
When, the innocent voices abating,
  Alert grow the innocent ears.

The little boys leap from the stairways,
  Girls lay down their dolls on the dot,
For promptly at five o'er the airways
  Comes violence geared to the tot.

Comes murder, comes arson, come G-men
  Pursuing unspeakable spies;
Come gangsters and tough-talking he-men
  With six-shooters strapped to their thighs;

Comes the corpse in the dust, comes the dictum
  "Ya' better start singin', ya' rat!"
While the torturer leers at his victim,
  The killer unleashes his gat.

With mayhem the twilight is reeling.
  Blood spatters, the tommy guns bark.
Hands reach for the sky or the ceiling
  As the dagger strikes home in the dark.

And lo! with what rapturous wonder
  The little ones hark to each tale
Of gambler shot down with his plunder
  Or outlaw abducting the mail.

Between the news and the tireless
  Commercials, while tempers turn sour,
Comes a season of horror by wireless,
  That is known as the Children's Hour.
                    —PHYLLIS McGINLEY

"The Children's Hour," a famous old poem by Henry Wadsworth Longfellow, has exactly the same first stanza as this poem. In his poem, Longfellow describes an hour of reading stories aloud to his grandchildren.

Why do you think Phyllis McGinley started her poem by quoting Longfellow's? The last stanza fits the rest of her poem better than the first stanza does. Why do you suppose she didn't start with it?

What would it be like to have an identical twin?

THE TWINS

In form and feature, face and limb,
    I grew so like my brother,
That folks got taking me for him,
    And each for one another.
It puzzled all our kith and kin,
    It reached a fearful pitch;
For one of us was born a twin,
    Yet not a soul knew which.

One day, to make the matter worse,
    Before our names were fixed,
As we were being washed by nurse,
    We got completely mixed;
And thus, you see, by fate's decree,
    Or rather nurse's whim,
My brother John got christened me,
    And I got christened him.

This fatal likeness even dogged
    My footsteps when at school,
And I was always getting flogged,
    For John turned out a fool.
I put this question, fruitlessly,
    To everyone I knew,
"What would you do, if you were me,
    To prove that you were you?"

Our close resemblance turned the tide
    Of my domestic life,
For somehow, my intended bride
    Became my brother's wife.
In fact, year after year the same
    Absurd mistakes went on,
And when I died, the neighbors came
    And buried brother John.

—HENRY S. LEIGH

Which of the confusions sounds the most serious to you? If you were a twin, how would you prove who you were?

Do people ever expect a person (not a twin) to be just like someone else in some way? What attitude do you think this poem is making fun of?

Which parts of a room are absolutely necessary? Could any part be missing, and the room still be a room?

THE CEILING

Suppose the Ceiling went Outside
And then caught Cold and Up and Died?
The only Thing we'd have for Proof
That he was Gone, would be the Roof;
I think it would be Most Revealing
To find out how the Ceiling's Feeling.

—THEODORE ROETHKE

Roethke talks about the ceiling as if it were a—what?

✓ ✓ ✓

I WISH THAT MY ROOM HAD A FLOOR

I wish that my room had a floor!
I don't so much care for a door,
　　But this crawling around
　　Without touching the ground
Is getting to be quite a bore!

—GELETT BURGESS

✓ ✓ ✓

How would a pig (or any other animal) feel about becoming meat for people to eat?

THE PIG

The pig, if I am not mistaken,
Supplies us sausage, ham, and bacon.
Let others say his heart is big—
I call it stupid of the pig.

—OGDEN NASH

Do you agree with the "others" or with the poet?

If you had a chance to interview an octopus, what would you ask him?

THE OCTOPUS

Tell me, O Octopus, I begs,
Is those things arms, or is they legs?
I marvel at thee, Octopus;
If I were thou, I'd call me Us.

—OGDEN NASH

Do you think the poet is offering the octopus good advice?
What pronouns in the poem are unusual in modern speech?
Why do you think the poet uses them?

Do adults ever act as if they were children?

FATHER WILLIAM

"You are old, Father William," the young man said,
"And your hair has become very white;
And yet you incessantly stand on your head—
Do you think, at your age, it is right?"

"In my youth," Father William replied to his son,
"I feared it might injure the brain;
But, now that I'm perfectly sure I have none,
Why, I do it again and again."

"You are old," said the youth, "as I mentioned before,
And have grown most uncommonly fat;
Yet you turned a back-somersault in at the door—
Pray, what is the reason of that?"

"In my youth," said the sage, as he shook his gray locks,
  "I kept all my limbs very supple
By the use of this ointment—one shilling the box—
  Allow me to sell you a couple?"

"You are old," said the youth, "and your jaws are too
    weak
  For anything tougher than suet;
Yet you finished the goose, with the bones and the beak—
  Pray how did you manage to do it?"

"In my youth," said his father, "I took to the law,
  And argued each case with my wife;
And the muscular strength which it gave to my jaw,
  Has lasted the rest of my life."

"You are old," said the youth, "one would hardly
    suppose
  That your eye was as steady as ever;
Yet you balanced an eel on the end of your nose—
  What made you so awfully clever?"

"I have answered three questions, and that is enough,"
  Said his father; "don't give yourself airs!
Do you think I can listen all day to such stuff?
  Be off, or I'll kick you downstairs."

—LEWIS CARROLL

Which of Father William's answers did you like best? What
kind of man does Father William seem to be?

Do you think Father William should have answered the last
question too? Why did he refuse to?

Haiku

Haiku can be a gentle way of making fun.

You hear that fat frog
   In the seat of
   Honor, singing
Bass? . . . That's the boss

—ISSA

What is the frog compared to? In how many ways could the two be alike?

✓ ✓ ✓

What could cause neighbors to be noisy?

O moon, why must you
inspire my neighbor to chirp
   all night on a flute!

—KOYO

Why do you think Koyo speaks to the moon rather than to his neighbor? What word imitates the flute? Would you like to hear that sound all night?

138

Sometimes a haiku writer speaks directly to his subject.

> If things were better
> for me, flies, I'd invite you
> to share my supper.
>
> —ISSA

What is Issa's attitude toward the flies? What does the poem show about his character?

✓ ✓ ✓

Have you ever looked at an insect's face? What did it look like?

> The face of the dragon-fly
> Is practically nothing
> But eyes.
>
> —CHISOKU

✓ ✓ ✓

> Now the man has a child
> He knows all the names
> Of the local dogs.
>
> —ANONYMOUS

Limericks

A limerick is a special kind of verse which always has the same shape. The name *limerick* probably came from a song which had a chorus starting, "Will you come up to Limerick?" Limerick is a town in Ireland.

There once was a man of Bengal
Who was asked to a Fancy Dress Ball;
    He murmured: "I'll risk it
    And go as a biscuit!"
But the dog ate him up in the hall.

                                    —ANONYMOUS

✓ ✓ ✓

There was an old man of Blackheath
Who sat on his set of false teeth.
    Said he, with a start,
    "O Lord, bless my heart!
I have bitten myself underneath!"

                                      —ANONYMOUS

✓ ✓ ✓

There once were two cats of Kilkenny,
Each thought there was one cat too many;
    So they fought and they fit,
    And they scratched and they bit,
Till instead of two cats there weren't any.

                                      —ANONYMOUS

An epicure, dining at Crewe,
Found quite a large mouse in his stew.
    Said the waiter, "Don't shout,
    And wave it about,
Or the rest will be wanting one, too!"

                         —ANONYMOUS

✓ ✓ ✓

RELATIVITY

There was a young lady named Bright,
Who traveled much faster than light.
    She started one day
    In a relative way
And returned on the previous night.

                         —ANONYMOUS

✓ ✓ ✓

From these examples, can you tell what the shape of a limerick
is? Which lines rhyme? How is one set of rhyming lines different
from the other set?

6

POEMS
EXPRESS
IDEAS

The world is full of ideas: ideas about different subjects, different ideas on the same subject. If you tried to think of all your ideas at once, your head would spin. And reading or hearing other people's ideas keeps giving you new ones. Although you may not agree with all the ideas you hear or read, trying to understand them can help you decide what *you* think.

Once you've decided, you may express your idea in words as well as in actions. Most often, you simply state an idea. "I can do my homework best to music," you may say. How might you say an opposite idea?

Then a friend tells you he can never get started on his homework because it's so quiet in his room. "Turn on the radio," you advise him. "Music will help you get started." How is this way of saying your idea different from simply stating it?

Sometimes you aren't sure of your idea. So you ask someone else what he thinks. Or perhaps you're sure, but you want to persuade someone else. A leading question will often help him to agree with you. "Don't you think it's better to study to music?" you ask your overnight guest, since you both have promised to finish your homework before you talk. When else might you choose to ask a question, rather than to state an idea directly?

A poem, too, may state an idea, advise you, or ask a question. The poet, like you, has reasons for choosing his way. You may notice a difference between his expression of an idea and your own expression of the same idea. But, as you learn to think and feel like a poet, you may soon be able to express your own ideas just as well as he expresses his.

Whether he states, advises, or asks a question, a poet often illustrates his expression of an idea. The illustration may set a scene or tell a story to help you understand the idea more clearly. Or it may picture the idea itself, just as another illustration may picture a feeling. Sometimes the illustrations in one poem do all these things.

Take the idea that words live, for instance. Choose a word that you think is lively, not dull and dead. What scene or what story would make a good background for saying that your word is alive? How might you picture the word itself? Would you choose a person or an animal or an object to picture a living word?

Have you ever looked in the mirror and wondered how your face became yours?

PHIZZOG

This face you got,
This here phizzog you carry around,
You never picked it out for yourself,
    at all, at all—did you?
This here phizzog—somebody handed it
    to you—am I right?
Somebody said, "Here's yours, now go see
    what you can do with it."
Somebody slipped it to you and it was like
    a package marked:
"No goods exchanged after being taken away"—
This face you got.

                            —CARL SANDBURG

How do you like the sound of "phizzog" as a word for "face"?

Does the person speaking in the poem know who assigns faces? What is he sure of? Is he right?

What can you tell about the speaker by the way he talks? Why do you think Sandburg chose this speaker to say the idea?

Write just one sentence, saying the main idea of "Phizzog" in the fewest words you can. How is your sentence different from the poem?

Why would a girl want to dye her hair?

FOR ANNE GREGORY

"Never shall a young man,
Thrown into despair
By those great honey-coloured
Ramparts at your ear,
Love you for yourself alone
And not your yellow hair."

"But I can get a hair-dye
And set such colour there,
Brown, or black, or carrot,
That young men in despair
May love me for myself alone
And not my yellow hair."

"I heard an old religious man
But yesternight declare
That he had found a text to prove
That only God, my dear,
Could love you for yourself alone
And not your yellow hair."

—WILLIAM BUTLER YEATS

Why does Anne Gregory want to dye her hair? Is her reason
a good one?

One of the speakers in this poem is evidently Anne Gregory
herself. Which lines does she say? Who might the other speaker be?
What hints does the poem give you?

What other things, besides good looks, are people liked for?
Do you think yellow hair, or the other things, can be separated
from the person himself?

BEAUTY

Beauty is seen
In the sunlight,
The trees, the birds,
Corn growing and people working
Or dancing for their harvest

Beauty is heard
In the night,
Wind sighing, rain falling,
Or a singer chanting
Anything in earnest.

Beauty is in yourself.
Good deeds, happy thoughts
That repeat themselves
In your dreams,
In your work,
And even in your rest.

—E-YEH-SHURE
(Louise Abeita)

146

Did you ever discover that something you believed wasn't true? How did your discovery make you feel?

IT DROPPED SO LOW—IN MY REGARD

It dropped so low—in my Regard—
I heard it hit the Ground—
And go to pieces on the Stones
At bottom of my Mind—

Yet blamed the Fate that flung it—*less*
Than I denounced Myself,
For entertaining Plated Wares
Upon my Silver Shelf—

—EMILY DICKINSON

What do you think dropped? What happened to it? What would break if it dropped on stones? What wouldn't break?

What caused it to fall? Why does the poet blame herself?

What is the difference between plated silver and pure silver? Dropping might not harm either one; which one, however, wears longer?

What else, besides silver, is most valuable if it is pure?

Why do people like the beach?

POEM

maggie and milly and molly and may
went down to the beach (to play one day)

and maggie discovered a shell that sang
so sweetly she couldn't remember her troubles, and

milly befriended a stranded star
whose rays five languid fingers were;

and molly was chased by a horrible thing
which raced sideways while blowing bubbles: and

may came home with a smooth round stone
as small as a world and as large as alone.

For whatever we lose (like a you or a me)
it's always ourselves we find in the sea

—E. E. CUMMINGS

Which girl would you choose to go to the beach with? Why would you choose her?

What did each girl find? Why do you suppose each one found a different thing in the same place? Why do you think the poet didn't capitalize all of their names?

What initial sounds of words are repeated? What is the starfish compared to indirectly? What diameter would you estimate for the stone that "may" found?

Which two lines of the poem say an idea? Do you agree with that idea? Why do you think Cummings told about the four girls, before saying the idea? How did each girl lose or find herself in the sea?

What keeps you from seeing what everyone in your class is doing? What prevents you from understanding how they all think and feel?

ALL BUT BLIND

All but blind
   In his chambered hole
Gropes for worms
   The four-clawed Mole.

All but blind
   In the evening sky,
The hooded Bat
   Twirls softly by.

All but blind
   In the burning day
The Barn-Owl blunders
   On her way.

And blind as are
   These three to me,
So, blind to Some-one
   I must be.

—WALTER DE LA MARE

Why do you think Walter de la Mare chose to write about the mole, the bat, and the barn-owl? What verbs show how these animals move? How are their movements similar?

Do you think the "Some-one" in the last stanza is an animal, a person, or someone else?

Do you agree with the idea of the poem? Is there someone you can't understand? Someone you can't sympathize with? Why can't you?

THE HIPPOPOTAMUS

Behold the hippopotamus!
We laugh at how he looks to us,
And yet in moments dank and grim
I wonder how we look to him.
Peace, peace, thou hippopotamus!
We really look all right to us,
As you no doubt delight the eye
Of other hippopotami.

—OGDEN NASH

✓ ✓ ✓

NIGHT THOUGHT
OF A
TORTOISE
SUFFERING FROM
INSOMNIA
ON A LAWN

The world is very flat—
There is no doubt of that.

—E. V. RIEU

Why does this poem need its title?

What if this were a daytime thought, not a night one? Or, if the tortoise were on a mountain peak, what might he decide about the world from that point of view? What might a deer awake on a lawn at night decide about the world?

150

THE SECRET SITS

We dance round in a ring and suppose,
But the Secret sits in the middle and knows.

—ROBERT FROST

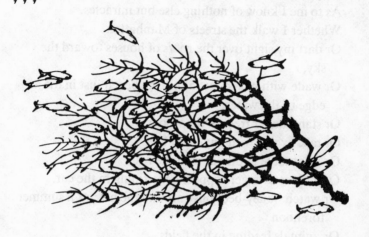

In Japan minnows were caught in tree branches, which were
placed to look as though they had fallen into the streams by chance.

Minnows are helpless
Caught in the branches of a tree
Set out to lure them,
So we too are tangled
In the snare of ignorance.

—LORD TOSHIYORI

According to the poet, when are people like minnows? Do you
agree?

Can minnows get out of their snare? Can people escape from
ignorance?

What might seem like a miracle to you?

MIRACLES

Why, who makes much of a miracle?
As to me I know of nothing else but miracles,
Whether I walk the streets of Manhattan,
Or dart my sight over the roofs of houses toward the
    sky,
Or wade with naked feet along the beach just in the
    edge of the water,
Or stand under trees in the woods,
Or talk by day with any one I love . . .
Or sit at table at dinner with the rest,
Or look at strangers opposite me riding in the car.
Or watch honey-bees busy around the hive of a summer
    forenoon,
Or animals feeding in the fields,
Or birds, or the wonderfulness of the sundown, or of
    stars shining so quiet and bright,
Or the exquisite delicate thin curve of the new moon
    in spring;
These with the rest, one and all, are to me miracles,
The whole referring, yet each distinct and in its place.

To me every hour of the light and dark is a miracle,
Every cubic inch of space is a miracle,
Every square yard of the surface of the earth is spread
    with the same,
Every foot of the interior swarms with the same.

To me the sea is a continual miracle,
The fishes that swim—the rocks—the motion of the
    waves—the ships with men in them,
What stranger miracles are there?

—WALT WHITMAN

What kinds of things does Walt Whitman see as miracles? Why might they seem miraculous to him? Do any of his miracles seem miraculous to you?

How would you answer the question at the end? Why do you think Walt Whitman asked the question: to find out what you think, or to persuade you?

Why should you choose your words carefully sometimes, rather than saying anything that pops into your head?

A WORD IS DEAD

A word is dead
When it is said,
Some say.

I say it just
Begins to live
That day.

—EMILY DICKINSON

PRIMER LESSON

Look out how you use proud words.
When you let proud words go, it is
    not easy to call them back.
They wear long boots, hard boots; they
    walk off proud; they can't hear you
    calling—
Look out how you use proud words.

—CARL SANDBURG

Why does the poet warn you about using proud words? Why do you think he calls his poem "*Primer* Lesson"?

How can words wear boots? What kind of boots? Why that kind?

Would Carl Sandburg agree with what Emily Dickinson says in "A Word Is Dead" or with what "some" say?

Besides describing or making fun gently, haiku can express an idea—sometimes by asking a question.

Wild geese O wild geese
 Were you little
 Fellows too . . . when
You flew from home?

         —ISSA

✓ ✓ ✓

The leaves never know
 Which leaf
 Will be first to fall . . .
Does the wind know?

        —SOSEKI

✓ ✓ ✓

But if I held it . . .
 Could I touch the
 Lightness of this
Flutter-butterfly?

         —BUSON

How do you think each poet intended his question to be answered? Who is each one asking?

What feeling about nature do all three questions express? Why is a question an appropriate way to express that feeling?

155

In my new clothing
   I feel so different
   I must
Look like someone else

—BASHO

When is it a pleasure for you to study or write? If you went to school in Japan, you might write with a brush rather than a pen.

It is a pleasure
When, spreading out some paper,
I take brush in hand
And write far more skillfully
Than I could have expected.

It is a pleasure
When, after a hundred days
Of twisting my words
Without success, suddenly
A poem turns out nicely.

—TACHIBANA AKEMI
(Translated by Donald Keene)

How are these two pleasures alike? Why would a poet enjoy both?

What is the main difference between the two pleasures? Do you think the poet enjoys one more than the other? Would you?

THE CHILD IN SCHOOL

Butterflies flit to and fro.
The herdboys are returning home.
Oh, blind old mister teacher,
Why don't you let me go?

—CHINESE FOLK SONG

7

POEMS MEAN THEMSELVES AND SOMETHING MORE

Practically everything in the world *can* mean itself and something more. Hitting a baseball means that your bat has connected with a ball thrown to you and that the bat has reversed the ball's direction. If the hit was a home run in the bottom of the ninth with two men out and the score tied, hitting the ball also means that you are a hero.

Being cheered as a hero means that you count. You've succeeded, and you have a right to be proud. Being proud of your skill means that you can be sure of yourself at school in other ways. What might being sure of yourself at school mean?

That one moment when you hit the home run could go on and on, meaning more and more. The high school baseball coach might take an interest in you and give you special help for the next few years. Then you might be offered a baseball scholarship to college or a contract with your favorite major-league team.

If you work backward in time from that moment, you could easily show how each successful stage of your practice meant itself at the time and something more, too. Now, taken all together, all your practice means your hit. But in looking back, what are you likely to do with the memory of the time you struck out, with the bases loaded and two outs for your side? How might even that failure have helped you succeed at last?

Practically everything you do and say, then, means itself and something more, somehow. Every object, too, means itself and something more. A bicycle means a two-wheeled vehicle; getting it as a gift may mean that someone is fond of you. The bicycle itself can additionally mean freedom to go places.

A poem, too, means itself and something more. What more and how much more depend on the poem and on you, the reader. To understand the meanings in a poem, it's a good idea first to see exactly what the poem itself says. Then you can go on to see further meanings as you think about the words of the poem.

Do you think everyone is likely to see exactly the same additional meaning as you do? Why might different people see different meanings in the same poem? Could even the heroic home run mean different things to different people?

What kind of letter might you start, "This is just to say . . ."?

THIS IS JUST TO SAY

I have eaten
the plums
that were in
the icebox

and which
you were probably
saving
for breakfast

Forgive me
they were delicious
so sweet
and so cold

—WILLIAM CARLOS WILLIAMS

Where might William Carlos Williams have left this poem? Would you forgive him if you found the note?

Which of the five senses does the last stanza appeal to? Which words in that stanza might you use to make a haiku about the plums?

What things might be delicious without necessarily being eatable? What good things might someone save, rather than use immediately? Which do you think is better: to save good things or to use them?

Why do you sometimes take time to put your belongings in order?

THE PASTURE

I'm going out to clean the pasture spring;
I'll only stop to rake the leaves away
(And wait to watch the water clear, I may):
I sha'n't be gone long.—You come too.

I'm going out to fetch the little calf
That's standing by the mother. It's so young
It totters when she licks it with her tongue.
I sha'n't be gone long.—You come too.

—ROBERT FROST

Would you like to come too? What in the invitation sounds appealing or unappealing to you?

Why would the pasture spring need to be cleaned? What other things need to be cleared out regularly?

Why does the calf need to be fetched in? What word most clearly pictures the reason? What other young animals sometimes need to be treated like the calf?

What kind of person is speaking in this poem? What clues about him does the poem give? Who might he be talking to?

Robert Frost put this poem at the beginning of the collection of all his poems. How might this invitation apply to readers of his poems? Judging from "The Pasture," what subjects would you guess many of his poems might be about?

The bat in *The Bat-Poet* wanted to make up a poem especially for his friends and relatives, the bats. Although he felt sleepy with winter coming on, he began to make a poem about a mother bat and her baby.

A BAT IS BORN

A bat is born
Naked and blind and pale.
His mother makes a pocket of her tail
And catches him. He clings to her long fur
By his thumbs and toes and teeth.
And then the mother dances through the night
Doubling and looping, soaring, somersaulting—
Her baby hangs on underneath.
All night, in happiness, she hunts and flies.
Her high sharp cries
Like shining needlepoints of sound
Go out into the night and, echoing back,
Tell her what they have touched.
She hears how far it is, how big it is,
Which way it's going:
She lives by hearing.
The mother eats the moths and gnats she catches
In full flight; in full flight
The mother drinks the water of the pond
She skims across. Her baby hangs on tight.
Her baby drinks the milk she makes him
In moonlight or starlight, in mid-air.
Their single shadow, printed on the moon
Or fluttering across the stars,
Whirls on all night; at daybreak
The tired mother flaps home to her rafter.
The others all are there.

They hang themselves up by their toes,
They wrap themselves in their brown wings.
Bunched upside down, they sleep in air.
Their sharp ears, their sharp teeth, their
    quick sharp faces
Are dull and slow and mild.
All the bright day, as the mother sleeps,
She folds her wings about her sleeping child.

—RANDALL JARRELL

What is it like to be a baby bat, according to this poem?

A bat has a natural radar system to guide its flight. What comparison in the poem shows you how the system works?

If you were an artist, commissioned to paint only one picture to illustrate this poem, which lines would you choose to illustrate? You would probably want to make the bats look like bats. At the same time, would you try to suggest something more?

✟ ✟ ✟

THE LAMB

The Lamb just says, I AM!
He frisks and whisks, *He* can.
He jumps all over. Who
Are *you*? You're jumping too!

—THEODORE ROETHKE

What does this lamb say? How does he say it?

What verbs show how the lamb moves? What do you notice about their sound?

Do you think the lamb thinks much before it jumps? Why do you think the poet capitalized "I AM!"? What kind of person is likely just to say, "I AM!"? What might he do to say it?

What might cause people to jump? Why do you think *He* and *you* are italicized? Are *you* jumping too?

How do fox and hounds run at the end of a hunt? How does the hunter ride?

HUNTING SONG

The fox came lolloping, lolloping,
Lolloping. His tongue hung out
And his ears were high.
He was like death at the end of a string
When he came to the hollow
Log. Ran in one side
And out of the other. O
He was sly.

The hounds came tumbling, tumbling,
Tumbling. Their heads were low
And their eyes were red.
The sound of their breath was louder than death
When they came to the hollow
Log. They held at one end
But a bitch found the scent. O
They were mad.

The hunter came galloping, galloping,
Galloping. All damp was his mare
From her hooves to her mane.
His coat and his mouth were redder than death
When he came to the hollow
Log. He took in the rein
And over he went. O
He was fine.

The log, he just lay there, alone in
The clearing. No fox nor hound
Nor mounted man
Saw his black round eyes in their perfect disguise
(As the ends of a hollow
Log). He watched death go through him,
Around him and over him. O
He was wise.

—DONALD FINKEL

What words tell how the fox, the hounds, and the hunter moved? How does the rhythm of the repeated words fit what is happening?

What details picture the fox? What details picture the hounds? Why do you think the poet pictured the horse, as well as the rider?

How do the comparisons in the first three stanzas suggest the fox's future? What senses do the comparisons appeal to?

What part does the log play? How is the rhythm of the last stanza different from the rhythm of the first three stanzas?

What word sums up the meaning of each of the participants in the hunt? Is each one behaving as you would expect him to? Which of the participants do you admire?

How do you react when you hear a cry of pain?

THE SNARE

I hear a sudden cry of pain!
   There is a rabbit in a snare:
Now I hear the cry again,
   But I cannot tell from where.

But I cannot tell from where
   He is calling out for aid;
Crying on the frightened air,
   Making everything afraid,

Making everything afraid
   Wrinkling up his little face,
As he cries again for aid;
   And I cannot find the place!

And I cannot find the place
   Where his paw is in the snare;
Little one! Oh, little one!
   I am searching everywhere.

                    —JAMES STEPHENS

How does the poet react to the cry of pain? What makes him think it's a rabbit, rather than some other animal? How can he know how the rabbit looks?

Where do the repeated lines occur? How does the repetition suggest the searcher's movements as he hunts for the rabbit?

Do you think he found the rabbit in time? Do you think he did right to try to find him?

Why might someone poison a mouse?

Me up at does

out of the floor
quietly Stare

a poisoned mouse

still who alive

is asking What
have i done that

You wouldn't have

—E. E. CUMMINGS

How does this mouse ask his question?

Say the words in the first four lines of the poem in an ordinary English sentence, starting with the subject: "A poisoned mouse . . ." What differences do you notice between the word order in the poem and that in the ordinary sentence? Why do you think the poet put the words in the order he did?

Which words are capitalized? Which usually capitalized word is not capitalized? Can you suggest any reasons for the capitalization or for the lack of it?

Why would someone poison a mouse? Why might other animals be poisoned? How else can animals be hurt? What justification might someone have for hurting an animal?

What might falling snow look like to someone who had never seen it?

CAT & THE WEATHER

Cat takes a look at the weather:
snow;
puts a paw on the sill;
his perch is piled, is a pillow.

Shape of his pad appears:
will it dig? No,
not like sand,
like his fur almost.

But licked, not liked:
too cold.
Insects are flying, fainting down.
He'll try

to bat one against the pane.
They have no body and no buzz,
and now his feet are wet;
it's a puzzle.

Shakes each leg,
then shakes his skin
to get the white flies off;
looks for his tail,

tells it to come on in
by the radiator.
World's turned queer
somehow: all white,

no smell. Well, here
inside it's still familiar.
He'll go to sleep until
it puts itself right.

—MAY SWENSON

What does Cat do to find out what snow is? Why does he reject each possibility he considers? Why can't he solve the puzzle?

Notice the length of lines in the first stanza. How does the line length suggest Cat's movements?

Which stanza has no punctuation at the end? What do you think is happening between that stanza and the next one?

How does Cat solve his puzzlement? Is his solution typical of cats? Do you think it's a good way to handle a hard problem?

What stories could you imagine about the moon?

who knows if the moon's
a balloon, coming out of a keen city
in the sky—filled with pretty people?
(and if you and i should

get into it, if they
should take me and take you into their balloon,
why then
we'd go up higher with all the pretty people

than houses and steeples and clouds:
go sailing
away and away sailing into a keen
city which nobody's ever visited, where

always
        it's
            Spring) and everyone's
in love and flowers pick themselves

—E. E. CUMMINGS

Where does the moon in the poem come from? Would you like
to take this balloon trip?

What adjectives are repeated? How precisely do they picture
the moon and its inhabitants? How do the other repeated words
suit the subject of the poem?

Does the season of the sky-city ever exist on earth? In what
ways? For how long? Would you like it to come and last forever?

A weeping child
Bids me
Pluck the full moon
From the sky.

—ISSA

WHAT THE RATTLESNAKE SAID

The moon's a little prairie-dog.
He shivers through the night.
He sits upon his hill and cries
For fear that *I* will bite.
The sun's a broncho. He's afraid
Like every other thing,
And trembles, morning, noon and night,
Lest *I* should spring, and sting.

—VACHEL LINDSAY

How long would it take a mouse to gnaw an oak tree down?

THE MOUSE THAT GNAWED
THE OAK-TREE DOWN

The mouse that gnawed the oak-tree down
Began his task in early life.
He kept so busy with his teeth
He had no time to take a wife.

He gnawed and gnawed through sun and rain
When the ambitious fit was on,
Then rested in the sawdust till
A month of idleness had gone.

He did not move about to hunt
The coteries of mousie-men.
He was a snail-paced, stupid thing
Until he cared to gnaw again.

The mouse that gnawed the oak-tree down,
When that tough foe was at his feet—
Found in the stump no angel-cake
Nor buttered bread, nor cheese nor meat—
The forest-roof let in the sky.
"This light is worth the work," said he.
"I'll make the ancient swamp more light,"
And started on another tree.

—VACHEL LINDSAY

172

How did the mouse manage to gnaw the oak tree down?

Did the poet think the mouse really expected to find angel cake, buttered bread, cheese, or meat inside the tree? What kinds of food are these? What might they stand for?

When someone says "Now I see the light," what kind of light does he mean? What do people sometimes do to "see the light"? Is the process anything like the way the mouse let in sunlight?

What way of living does this fable suggest? Do you agree with the suggestion?

✓ ✓ ✓

AT HERON LODGE

Mountains cover the white sun,
And oceans drain the golden river;
But you widen your view three hundred miles
By going up one flight of stairs.

—WANG CHIH-HUAN

Do you think it would be a pleasure to be at Heron Lodge? What can you see from there? What are the colors of the landscape?

What kind of statement usually follows the word *but*? Why does the third line start with "But . . ."? What is special about a three-hundred-mile view?

A political candidate might be asked about his views on education. What does the word *view* mean then? How else could you widen your view spectacularly, besides going up a flight of stairs?

THE WALRUS AND THE CARPENTER

The sun was shining on the sea,
   Shining with all his might:
He did his very best to make
   The billows smooth and bright—
And this was odd, because it was
   The middle of the night.

The moon was shining sulkily,
   Because she thought the sun
Had got no business to be there
   After the day was done—
"It's very rude of him," she said,
   "To come and spoil the fun!"

The sea was wet as wet could be,
   The sands were dry as dry.
You could not see a cloud, because
   No cloud was in the sky:
No birds were flying overhead—
   There were no birds to fly.

The Walrus and the Carpenter
   Were walking close at hand;
They wept like anything to see
   Such quantities of sand:
"If this were only cleared away,"
   They said, "it *would be* grand!"

"If seven maids with seven mops
     Swept it for half a year,
Do you suppose," the Walrus said,
     "That they could get it clear?"
"I doubt it," said the Carpenter,
     And shed a bitter tear.

"O Oysters, come and walk with us!"
     The Walrus did beseech.
"A pleasant walk, a pleasant talk,
     Along the briny beach:
We cannot do with more than four,
     To give a hand to each."

The eldest Oyster looked at him,
     But not a word he said:
The eldest Oyster winked his eye,
     And shook his heavy head—
Meaning to say he did not choose
     To leave the oyster-bed.

But four young Oysters hurried up,
     All eager for the treat:
Their coats were brushed, their faces washed,
     Their shoes were clean and neat—
And this was odd, because, you know,
     They hadn't any feet.

Four other Oysters followed them,
    And yet another four;
And thick and fast they came at last,
    And more, and more, and more—
All hopping through the frothy waves,
    And scrambling to the shore.

The Walrus and the Carpenter
    Walked on a mile or so,
And then they rested on a rock
    Conveniently low:
And all the little Oysters stood
    And waited in a row.

"The time has come," the Walrus said,
    "To talk of many things:
Of shoes—and ships—and sealing wax—
    Of cabbages—and kings—
And why the sea is boiling hot—
    And whether pigs have wings."

"But wait a bit," the Oysters cried,
    "Before we have our chat;
For some of us are out of breath,
    And all of us are fat!"
"No hurry!" said the Carpenter.
    They thanked him much for that.

"A loaf of bread," the Walrus said,
    "Is what we chiefly need:
Pepper and vinegar besides
    Are very good indeed—
Now, if you're ready, Oysters dear,
    We can begin to feed."

"But not on us!" the Oysters cried,
    Turning a little blue.
"After such kindness that would be
    A dismal thing to do!"
"The night is fine," the Walrus said,
    "Do you admire the view?"

"It was so kind of you to come,
    And you are very nice!"
The Carpenter said nothing but
    "Cut us another slice.
I wish you were not quite so deaf—
    I've had to ask you twice!"

"It seems a shame," the Walrus said,
    "To play them such a trick.
After we've brought them out so far
    And made them trot so quick!"
The Carpenter said nothing but
    "The butter's spread too thick!"

"I weep for you," the Walrus said,
   "I deeply sympathize."
With sobs and tears he sorted out
   Those of the largest size,
Holding his pocket-handkerchief
   Before his streaming eyes.

"O Oysters," said the Carpenter,
   "You've had a pleasant run!
Shall we be trotting home again?"
   But answer came there none—
And this was scarcely odd, because
   They'd eaten every one.

                              —LEWIS CARROLL

DIGGING FOR CHINA

"Far enough down is China," somebody said.
"Dig deep enough and you might see the sky
As clear as at the bottom of a well.
Except it would be real—a different sky.
Then you could burrow down until you came
To China! Oh, it's nothing like New Jersey.
There's people, trees, and houses, and all that,
But much, much different. Nothing looks the same."

I went and got the trowel out of the shed
And sweated like a coolie all that morning,
Digging a hole beside the lilac-bush,
Down on my hands and knees. It was a sort

Of praying, I suspect. I watched my hand
Dip deep and darker, and I tried and tried
To dream a place where nothing was the same.
The trowel never did break through to blue.

Before the dream could weary of itself
My eyes were tired of looking into darkness,
My sunbaked head of hanging down a hole.
I stood up in a place I had forgotten,
Blinking and staggering while the earth went round
And showed me silver barns, the fields dozing
In palls of brightness, patens growing and gone
In the tides of leaves, and the whole sky china blue.
Until I got my balance back again
All that I saw was China, China, China.

—RICHARD WILBUR

The "I" in this poem might have been the poet himself when
he was a boy. Why did he try to dig to China? Would you be
interested in seeing what he set out to see? What other things do
people often do for similar reasons?

How hard did the boy work? How was the way he worked
like praying?

Why did he quit digging? Had he given up hope of finding his
dream? Which words tell you how he felt when he stood up?

How could barns appear to be silver? A pall is a rich cloth,
often a cover for church altars, and a paten is a thin plate of
precious metal, used in communion in many churches. What would
make the fields appear to be covered with a rich cloth and the trees
seem to be filled with shining plate-like disks? What does the
appearance of the barns, fields, and trees tell you about the boy's
feelings or his physical condition?

How had the boy succeeded or not succeeded in doing what he
set out to do? Do people sometimes succeed or fail in the same
way?

Frontier life could be cruel for both men and animals.

THE WOLVES

Last night knives flashed. LeChien cried
And chewed blood in his bed.
Vanni's whittling blade
Had found flesh easier than wood.

Vanni and I left camp on foot. In a glade
We came on a brown blossom
Great and shining on a thorned stem.
"That's the sensitive briar," I said.

"It shrinks at the touch," I added.
Soon we found buffalo. Picking
A bull grazing by itself, I began
The approach: while the shaggy head

Was turned I sprinted across the sod,
And when he swung around his gaze
I bellyflopped in the grass
And lay on my heartbeat and waited.

When he looked away again I made
Enough yardage before he wheeled
His head: I kneeled, levelled
My rifle, and we calmly waited.

It occurred to me as we waited
That in those last moments he was,
In fact, daydreaming about something else.
"He is too stupid to live," I said.

His legs shifted and the heart showed.
I fired. He looked, trotted off,
He simply looked and trotted off,
Stumbled, sat himself down, and became dead.

I looked for Vanni. Amid the cows he stood,
Only his arms moving as he fired,
Loaded, and fired, the dumb herd
Milling about him sniffing at their dead.

I called and he retreated.
We cut two choice tongues for ourselves
And left the surplus. All day wolves
Would splash blood from those great sides.

Again we saw the flower, brown-red
On a thorn-spiked stem. When Vanni
Extended his fingers, it was funny,
It shrank away as if it had just died.

They told us in camp that LeChien was dead.
None of us cared. Nobody much
Had liked him. His tobacco pouch,
I observed, was already missing from beside his bed.

—GALWAY KINNELL

What are the two stories in this poem? Why do you think the poet put them both into the same poem?

What reasons could Vanni have had for killing so many buffalo cows? How does he seem to feel about any kind of killing?

How does the narrator ("I") kill? What reason does the narrator give for killing the bull? Is it a good reason? Why do you think he bothers to think of it?

What would happen to the slaughtered buffalo cows? What happened to LeChien's possessions? Who are "The Wolves"?

Would the briar have shrunk away from the narrator if he had reached out to it? How are the narrator and Vanni alike? How are they different?

How do you think the poet wanted his readers to react to the story?

What kinds of songs does America sing?

I HEAR AMERICA SINGING

I hear America singing, the varied carols I hear,
Those of mechanics, each one singing his as it should
   be blithe and strong,
The carpenter singing his as he measures his plank
   or beam,
The mason singing his as he makes ready for work, or
   leaves off work,
The boatman singing what belongs to him in his boat,
   the deckhand singing on the steamboat deck,
The shoemaker singing as he sits on his bench, the
   hatter singing as he stands,
The wood-cutter's song, the ploughboy's on his way in
   the morning, or at noon intermission or at sundown,
The delicious singing of the mother, or of the young
   wife at work, or of the girl sewing or washing,
Each singing what belongs to him or her and to none
   else,
The day what belongs to the day—at night the party
   of young fellows, robust, friendly,
Singing with open mouths their strong melodious songs.
                                        —WALT WHITMAN

How are these songs alike? How are the singers alike?
Are there people in America doing other jobs besides those
Walt Whitman mentions? Why do you think he says he hears
America singing?

THE PEASANT AND THE SHEEP

A Peasant had a Sheep indicted
And brought to trial for a heinous crime.
The judge, a Fox, was not one to waste time.
He told both parties: "Now, without getting excited
And shouting at each other, tell the Court just what
    took place.
Include all evidence material to the case."

The Peasant testified: "On such-and-such a date,
One of my hens was missing. On the ground
I saw some bones and feathers. And I hereby state
That Sheep, there, was the only one around."

"I'm innocent, Your Honor," said the Sheep.
"Just ask my friends: they'll tell you I was fast asleep
That whole night. Anyway who ever heard
Of a lamb committing larceny
Plus murder in the first degree?
Besides, I never eat the flesh of beast or bird."

Here is Judge Fox's ruling, word for word:
"The Court finds it cannot accept
Sheep's arguments. These clever thieves are most adept,
I can assure you, at making someone else their dupe.
Also, as Plaintiff's testimony shows,
Sheep spent that whole night near the chicken coop.

Now, hens are very tasty, as everybody knows;
Thus tempted, anyone would drool.
The question is, in short:
Could Defendant have desisted from devouring the
    Deceased?

Obviously not. Therefore, I rule

That Sheep, whose guilt is evident, be put to death and fleeced,

His wool assigned to Plaintiff, and his carcass to the Court."

—IVAN ANDREEVICH KRYLOV
(translated by Guy Daniels)

✓ ✓ ✓

THE SWAN, THE CRAB, AND THE PIKE

A Swan, a Sand-Crab, and a Pike, one day,
Made up their minds to pull a cart of hay.
When all three had been harnessed up, the Swan said,
  "Start!"
They labored mightily, but couldn't budge the cart.
Why not? It was a light load, and not awkward.
But the Swan kept trying to fly;
The Pike, finding dry land a bit *too* dry,
Flopped toward a pond nearby;
And the Crab went backward.

Now, who was right and who was wrong in this affair,
I know not. But the cart's still there.

—IVAN ANDREEVICH KRYLOV
(translated by Guy Daniels)

✓ ✓ ✓

Most people are fascinated by nests of boxes. You open one box, and inside is another one. When it is opened, there is yet another. When will you reach the last one? How small can a box be?

THIS IS THE KEY

This is the Key of the Kingdom:
In that Kingdom is a city;
In that city is a town;
In that town there is a street;
In that street there winds a lane;
In that lane there is a yard;
In that yard there is a house;
In that house there waits a room;
In that room an empty bed;
And on that bed a basket—
A Basket of Sweet Flowers:
Of Flowers, of Flowers;
A Basket of Sweet Flowers.

Flowers in a Basket;
Basket on the bed;
Bed in the chamber;
Chamber in the house;
House in the weedy yard;
Yard in the winding lane;
Lane in the broad street;
Street in the high town;
Town in the city;
City in the Kingdom—
This is the Key of the Kingdom;
Of the Kingdom this is the Key.

—ANONYMOUS

What is the Key to the Kingdom? How do you reach the statement of what it is? Why do you think the poem didn't give the Key in the first line?

What kind of Kingdom could have a basket of flowers as its Key?

What other imaginary kingdoms could possibly exist today? What might be the key to an imaginary kingdom? What layers hide the key from sight?

THE CLOSING OF THE RODEO

The lariat snaps; the cowboy rolls
   His pack, and mounts and rides away.
Back to the land the cowboy goes.

Plumes of smoke from the factory sway
   In the setting sun. The curtain falls,
A train in the darkness pulls away.

Goodbye, says the rain on the iron roofs.
   Goodbye, say the barber poles.
Dark drum the vanishing horses' hooves.

—WILLIAM JAY SMITH

ACKNOWLEDGMENTS (continued from page iv)

Doubleday & Company, Inc.: For "The Bat," copyright 1938, 1939; "Child on Top of a Greenhouse," copyright 1946 by Editorial Publications, Inc., from *Words for the Wind* by Theodore Roethke. Reprinted by permission of Doubleday & Company, Inc. For "The Ceiling," copyright 1950; "The Gnu," copyright © 1961; "The Kitty-Cat Bird," "The Lamb," "Old Florist," copyright 1946 by Harper & Brothers, all from *I Am! Says the Lamb*, by Theodore Roethke. Reprinted by permission of Doubleday & Company, Inc. For "freddy the rat perishes" from *Archy and Mehitabel* by Don Marquis. Copyright 1927 by Doubleday & Company, Inc. Reprinted by permission of the publisher. For "Little Elegy," copyright © 1960 by X. J. Kennedy, from *Nude Descending a Staircase* by X. J. Kennedy. (Originally appeared in *The New Yorker*.) Reprinted by permission of Doubleday & Company, Inc. For "Insects one hears" by Wafū, from *An Introduction to Haiku* by Harold G. Henderson, copyright © 1958 by Harold G. Henderson. Reprinted by permission of Doubleday & Company, Inc.

Gerald Duckworth and Co., Limited: For "Overheard on a Saltmarsh" from *Collected Poems* (in preparation) by Harold Monro, by permission of Mrs. Alida Monro and Gerald Duckworth and Co., Limited.

E. P. Dutton & Co., Inc.: For "The Flattered Flying Fish" and "Night Thought of a Tortoise" from *The Flattered Flying Fish and Other Poems* by E. V. Rieu. Copyright, ©, 1962 by E. V. Rieu. Reprinted by permission of E. P. Dutton & Co., Inc. For "I Wish That My Room Had a Floor" by Gelett Burgess, from *A Century of Humorous Verse*, edited by Roger L. Green. Everyman's Library. Reprinted by permission of E. P. Dutton & Co., Inc.

Mrs. Norma Millay Ellis: For "Lament" and "Portrait by a Neighbour" from *Collected Poems* by Edna St. Vincent Millay, Harper & Row. Copyright 1921, 1922, 1928, 1948, 1950, 1955 by Edna St. Vincent Millay and Norma Millay Ellis.

Ernst, Cane, Berner & Gitlin, Counsellors: For "Nursery Rhyme for the Tender-Hearted" by Christopher Morley.

Faber & Faber Ltd.: For "maggie and milly and molly and may" and "who knows if the moon's" from *Selected Poems* by E. E. Cummings. For "n," "may i be gay," "Me up at does," "e" from *73 Poems* by E. E. Cummings. For "Digging for China" from *Poems, 1943–1956* by Richard Wilbur.

Farrar, Straus & Giroux, Inc.: For "The Closing of the Rodeo," reprinted from *Celebration at Dark* by William Jay Smith, by permission of Farrar, Straus & Giroux, Inc.

Grove Press, Inc.: For "It is a pleasure" by Tachibana Akemi, translated by Donald Keene, from *Anthology of Japanese Literature: From the Earliest Era to the Mid-Nineteenth Century*, compiled and edited by Donald Keene, published by Grove Press, Inc.. copyright © 1955 by Grove Press.

Hallmark Cards, Incorporated: For "The face of the dragon-fly" by Chisoku and "The long night" by Shiki, from *Haiku*, by R. H. Blyth, © Hallmark Cards, Incorporated: Reprinted by permission of Hokuseido Press, Tokyo. and Hallmark Cards, Incorporated.

Hamish Hamilton Ltd.: For "The Closing of the Rodeo" from *Celebration at Dark* by William Jay Smith. Published in the British Empire by Hamish Hamilton Ltd.

Harcourt, Brace & World, Inc.: For "A spark in the sun" by Harry Behn, "How cool cut hay smells" by Boncho, "Frog-school competing" by Shiki, "An old silent pond" by Basho, "One man and one fly" and "If things were better" by Issa, "Oh moon, why must you" by Koyo, from *Cricket Songs: Japanese Haiku*, translated and © 1964, by Harry Behn. Reprinted by per-